Kari Torjesen Malcolm

BUILDING YOUR FAMILY TO LAST

INTERVARSITY PRESS
DOWNERS GROVE, ILLINOIS 60515

InterVarsity Press is the book-publishing division of InterVarsity Christian Fellowship, a student movement active on campus at hundreds of universities, colleges and schools of nursing. For information about local and regional activities, write Public Relations Dept., InterVarsity Christian Fellowship, 6400 Schroeder Rd., P.O. Box 7895, Madison, WI 53707-7895.

Distributed in Canada through InterVarsity Press, 860 Denison St., Unit 3, Markham, Ontario L3R 4H1, Canada.

All Scripture quotations, unless otherwise indicated, are from the Revised Standard Version of the Bible, copyrighted 1946, 1952, 1971 by the Division of Christian Education of the National Council of Churches of Christ in the U.S.A., and are used by permission. All rights reserved.

Cover photograph: Michael Goss

The quotation on page 98 from "O Lord, You're Beautiful" by Keith Green is © 1980 by Birdwing Music/ Cherry Lane Music Publishing Co., Inc. (Admin. by The Sparrow Corporation, 9255 Deering Avenue, Chatsworth, CA 91311). All rights reserved. International copyright secured. Used by permission.

ISBN 0-87784-984-6

Printed in the United States of America

Library of Congress Cataloging-in-Publication Data

Malcolm, Kari Torjesen, 1925-
    Building your family to last.

    Bibliography: p.
    1. Family—United States.   2. Family—United States—
Religious life.   3.   Parent and child—United States.
I. Title.
HQ535.M35   1987   306.8'5'0973   87-3426
ISBN 0-87784-984-6

17	16	15	14	13	12	11	10	9	8	7	6	5	4	3	2	1
99	98	97	96	95	94	93	92	91	90	89	88	87				

To our children,
Kirsten and O-i,
who have given us the highest joy
as they have, with their families,
accepted the torch of freedom to
continue without interruption
the family adventure
of many generations
to the City of God.

Acknowledgments

Special recognition goes to my
editor, Joan Lloyd Guest,
who has assisted me in the
birthing of my first two books:
this one and Women at the
Crossroads. *I am grateful for*
the deep friendship that has
resulted from our
collaboration in these
writing projects.

Another friend—Jim Nyquist—
got me started with
InterVarsity Press when he was
director by encouraging me to
submit my first book. How
grateful I am for a brother
who gave me hope when I was
just a fledgling writer,
uncertain of my wings. Thank
you, Jim, for giving
me courage!

1

THE FAMILY'S JOURNEY OF FAITH

WHEN MY FATHER FIRST SAILED to China as a missionary, he chose as his life motto Paul's words: "It is my eager expectation and hope that I shall not be at all ashamed, but that with full courage now as always Christ will be honored in my body, whether by life or by death" (Phil 1:20).

He was a pilgrim setting off for an unknown land. After six weeks on a ship, he spent two weeks on the back of a mule before reaching his destination—a city on the border of Shanxi and Inner Mongolia where the gospel of Jesus Christ had never been heard, and where twenty-one years later he would lay down his life.

As he left Norway, the outward journey in time and space was fused with the inward journey of following Christ to the City of God. His goal of reaching that city was just as real to him as the goal of reaching China. He could have stayed on in Kristiansand, Norway, and gone into business like some of his brothers. But somehow his journey took a different route. Like Abraham, he "obeyed when he was called to go out to a place which he was to receive as an inheritance; and he went out, not knowing where he was to go. By faith he sojourned in a land of promise, as in a foreign land. . . . For he looked forward to the city which has foundations, whose builder and maker is God" (Heb 11:8-10).

Although my parents were engaged when my father left for China, they were not able to be together immediately. The China Inland Mission set up by Hudson Taylor treated married men and women as equal partners in mission. Therefore, each needed training, including two years of intensive language study. Before my mother and father could be married, she had to finish her missionary education in Oslo and London and then take two years of Chinese in China (far from my father's lonely post).

But to my parents these four years apart were treated as just the natural course of events as they proceeded on their pilgrimage to the City of God. All things were viewed from the perspective of being pilgrims on the road to the kingdom. When my brothers and I came along we became a family of pilgrims. And because the concept of a pilgrimage was so much a part of our family life, John Bunyan's great book *A Pilgrim's Progress* became one of our favorites.[1]

A Family of Pilgrims

By modeling the journey of faith and love for us, my parents gave us an inheritance that millionaires cannot buy. They gave us a world view that prepared us to face each day with courage while keeping our eyes on the goal of some day reaching the City of God.

"Ah'm tired of livin', an' scared of dyin'," was never a sentiment expressed at our home. There was a thrill and excitement about exploring a new land to be invaded for Jesus Christ, and at the same time there was a fearlessness if the adventure should lead to death. Death had lost its sting. My earliest memories about death were that it was something to look forward to with joy because Jesus would welcome the pilgrims at the gate of the City of God.[2]

And so, thrilled with life and unafraid of death, we learned to live as a pilgrim family with some very specific goals. There was the inward goal of becoming like Christ by learning to love God and hate sin. My parents modeled this for us, as well as the outward goal of loving others at the expense of oneself.

Today, many families are in trouble because their goals have been misplaced. They wander aimlessly through life, having no goals at all or focusing on goals such as success or wealth, which tend to split the family apart, not draw it together.

This book is about families and how they can be saved in this age of divorce and disillusionment. We save the family, not by focusing on it, but by focusing on Christ so that parents become models of discipleship to their children (Heb 12:1-2). That's what my parents were to me as we lived lives of pilgrims in China.

The Way of the Wanderer

In sharp contrast to the life of the pilgrim stands the life of the wanderer. The longer the wanderer travels, the more vague his goals become. Meanwhile, because he makes no commitments to either God or other people, he becomes more and more alienated from others and cut off from his roots.

Henrik Ibsen's Peer Gynt is a prime example in literature of a drifter, a hollow man who has spent his life plagued by the problems of identity and values. He says about himself at the end of his life of wandering, "So unspeakably poor then, a soul can go back to nothingness in the misty gray."[3]

Peer Gynt is a man who has followed the Troll Motto: "Troll, to yourself be enough."[4] He has never cared for anyone else all of his life. When Peer Gynt finally returns to Norway to die, Ibsen dramatizes his selfish and fragmented life by letting the hero hear the funeral sermon for a dead farmer. The honored dead man becomes Peer's alter ego as Peer hears the story of a man who has lived selflessly, devoting his strength to raising three God-fearing, industrious sons.

The farmer had lived on the highest crag of a mountain, the only place he had to make a living for his family. Eager for his sons to go to school to get an education and to learn their catechism, the farmer each morning and afternoon roped the youngest son in front of him and the second on his back, while tying another rope to the eldest son, so that going down to school or returning, the boys were roped to their father for safety.[5]

The rope became a rope of love tying this family of mountain dwellers together. Like my own father, this man was a model of selfless love to his family. Each day took him on another journey of love as he risked his life to give his family the best he could give them. As Peer listened to the pastor's eulogy, he saw the contrast between his own life and that of his alter ego.

None of us can measure our wealth when we have grown up with parents who have been models of selfless love in their relationship to God, to us and to others. By contrast, parents who have not been good models for their children tend to beget children who will fail to be models for the next generation, and the next—and the next!

Using God's Gifts

By following Jesus in self-denial and sacrifice (Jn 3:16 and 15:13), we will build a foundation for our families to grow and thrive together. Jesus' call to discipleship comes to us today as a call to save our family by the age-old principle of laying down our lives for others (Mt 16:24).

"But won't you gyp your own family in the process?" I have been asked over and over again. No, because our capacity to love grows with the number of people we take into our hearts and homes. Love is a great gift of God—given to us, not in limited quantities or chunks, but in abundance. I don't have to choose between loving my own family, loving a refugee family, or loving a group of foreign students. Instead, the more love I give away, the more love is given to me from God's inexhaustible supply, for "God is love" (1 Jn 4:8; Rom 5:5).

The following hymn is one we frequently sang while I was growing up in China. It speaks of the power God gives us for the journey of faith—for being Christ's disciples and for being the disciplers of our families:

Guide me, O Thou great Jehovah,
Pilgrim through this barren land;
I am weak, but Thou art mighty;
Hold me with Thy powerful hand;
Bread of heaven, bread of heaven,
Feed me till I want no more,
Feed me till I want no more.

Open now the crystal fountain,
Whence the healing waters flow;
Let the fire and cloudy pillar,
Lead me all my journey through:
Strong Deliverer, strong deliverer,
Be Thou still my strength and shield;
Be Thou still my strength and shield.[6]

The hymn writer reminds us of God's people wandering through the desert to the Promised Land, eating the manna from heaven. Jesus compared himself to that manna: "I am the living bread which came down from heaven. . . . He who eats my flesh and drinks my blood has eternal life" (Jn 6:51, 54). At the Lord's Table, as well as in the moment-by-moment communion we have with God through prayer and meditation on his Word, we are being fed for the journey of faith. In that spiritual food we find the power to become models of faith for our children. We cannot become such models if we are spiritually dying of hunger and thirst.

When we take our food from God, we find that we have strength enough for the journey of faith, for our families, and for others as well. We have food for the needy, a message of hope for the hopeless, and a message of salvation for all. And most importantly, we have a goal, a direction in life which unifies our family in ministry together.

The Enemy Within and Without

Many people today talk about the forces in society which threaten to tear families apart. But I believe that the forces outside the family—poverty, oppression, war, disease, stress— are not nearly so dangerous as the forces inside—anger, power struggles, sexual infidelity, emotional breakdown, uncertainty, and so on.

During the war years in China, the outside forces which threatened our family were very real. My father was killed when our home was bombed, and we were imprisoned under physically difficult conditions. We four children didn't have a father during the years when we needed one most. But my father didn't desert us. He risked his life and died as a shepherd who refused to desert his flock in the hour of their greatest need. This heroic self-sacrifice took the sting out of his death, for "greater love has no man than this, that a man lay down his life for his friends" (Jn 15:13).

It's hard to explain why the four of us were not more scarred and wounded by these experiences. But what happened on the outside intensified rather than destroyed our family unity. We had each other. The same was true of the children who stayed with their parents in London during the World War 2 bombings. Those children were less traumatized than the ones who were sent to homes out in the countryside to protect them.

War between nations is never as terrifying to a child as the war within our four walls—the war that destroys loving relationships right in the sanctuary of the home. The real problems are to be found in our hearts and homes, so that's where the solution has to be found as well, it seems to me.

Many secular sociologists and psychologists are agreeing with

Christians that the root of the problems of juvenile delinquency and criminality start in childhood in homes that do not provide the love and nurture and modeling that the child needs.

Many of us prefer to blame such family breakdown on all the evil influences in the world around us. But I think the reverse is true. Our Western civilization is disintegrating because of the breakdown of the family, the primary unit of society. And the family is falling apart because the married couple that's trying to keep the home together do not know their identity or destination—because there were no models in the families they came from. Therefore, they are unable to build a strong Christian home of love and support. With all their idealism and love for each other, there is a tragic flaw: because they had no models, they are unable to become models to the next generation.

But are we stuck in this cycle of inadequate relationships? Where is our hope? As we recognize that the problem that started in the heart and the home has to be solved there, we do well to heed the call that the apostle James made almost 2,000 years ago to people with similar problems:

What causes wars, and what causes fighting among you? Is it not your passions that are at war in your members? You desire and do not have; so you kill. And you covet and cannot obtain; so you fight and wage war. . . . Do you not know that friendship with the world is enmity with God? Therefore whoever wishes to be a friend of the world makes himself an enemy of God. . . . Submit . . . to God. Resist the devil. . . . Draw near to God and he will draw near to you. Cleanse your hands, you sinners, and purify your hearts. (Jas 4:1-2, 4, 7-8)

James gives a call to repentance, and that's what this book is all about. Because of God's grace every family can make a 180-degree turn and find a new identity and destiny as a family of pilgrims. No family has to become a victim of the enemies outside and inside the home. But there will be no easy answers or formulas for success, for the journey of faith is not completed in ten easy steps. We go out not knowing the next step, but looking toward the holy city, "which has foundations, whose builder and maker is God" (Heb 11:10).

During the three years of prison camp after my father's death, we were on a journey of faith together to the City of God where my father had gone ahead of us. The deep love and loyalty that existed between us, as well as our faith in a good God, sustained us:

For the mountains may depart
　　and the hills be removed,
but my steadfast love shall not
　　depart from you,
and my covenant of peace shall
　　not be removed,
says the LORD, who has
　　compassion on you. (Is 54:10)

2

MARRIAGE:
THE START

As I GREW UP IN CHINA, I WAS taught by my parents and others in the missionary community that when it comes to marriage there are only two alternatives: Either follow in the steps of Jesus and remain single, or enter into Christian marriage with the aim to astound a world that has grown to expect unhappiness and brokenness. There are no other options, I was told.

So when my turn came to give advice, I counseled my teen-aged children that marriage and singleness are a 50-50 proposition. You can be single for the Lord and find fulfillment, or you can be married for the Lord and find fulfillment. But you cannot compromise your identity or destiny as a child of God and find fulfillment.

The more I am united to Christ in deep love, the more I will love my husband and children, and this life of caring will spill over into the world. When the kingdom of God is my first concern, my priorities will be such that my marriage and family will thrive.

But when our eyes are distracted from Christ, when our vision of the City of God falters, then we run the risk of making decisions which will lead to the destruction of the family. Today, many factors work against building strong marriages. And many of these factors arise during courtship. The decision to marry may be made prematurely or for the wrong reasons. And that leads to difficulties later on.

Starry-Eyed Romance

Psychologist Scott Peck writes insightfully about what it means to fall in love. Falling in love, he points out, is always a "sex-linked, erotic experience . . . [which] is invariably temporary."[1] When we first meet that special person the sexual, emotional and interpersonal dynamics are such that we can think of no one or nothing else. Our lives are full of fireworks and grand weddings. Rational thinking and thoughtful decision making tend to be difficult in those high-energy days. As Peck describes it, there is a temporary collapse of our ego boundaries—a complete end to loneliness at last.

But because we are indeed two individuals, not one, our ego boundaries inevitably re-exert themselves. We become again two separate people, and we fall out of love. At this point we either begin to dissolve the bonds of the relationship, of the marriage, or we initiate the task of real loving—as two persons.[2]

What Peck means by real love is the love that apart from feelings decides to act lovingly. This involves the will, while falling "in love" is effortless: "We are as likely to fall in love with someone with whom we are obviously ill matched as with someone more suitable. Indeed, we may not even admire the object of our passion."[3]

It's in those initial days of romance that some of the first mistakes are made by couples. Many Christians have not been taught about the strength of sexual drives and the influence of romantic feelings on their desire to marry. They think that the desire is enough on which to build a relationship that will last a lifetime. But later the new husband and wife may find themselves married to someone who is very different from themselves. And the more different the two are the harder it will be for them to build a strong bond. (But it is never impossible.)

There are three areas in which couples may face difficulty because they have married someone with whom they have little in common. First, they may marry someone who is not their spiritual equal. We do not need a special message from God to tell us that two people who are walking on two separate roads and going in different directions will have a hard time walking together. The Bible puts it this way: "Do not be mismated with unbelievers. For what partnership have righteousness and iniquity? Or what fellowship has light with darkness? . . . Or what has a believer in common with an unbeliever? . . . For we are the temple of the living God" (2 Cor 6:14-16).

But in an age of tolerance, when the faith of a prospective bride or groom is questioned, the response is that we have no right to judge. How do we know what is going on in his or her heart? Then comes a litany of outward Christian duties the person in question has performed—from "going forward to accept Christ as Savior" to having been baptized, catechized and confirmed. But we all know how easy it is to go through the motions of these events and miss the kingdom of God. Too many young people get married in the hope that the beloved one will grow a lot spiritually—or will make Christ lord—after the wedding.

Those who have married someone who is spiritually unequal will face the hardship of being the spiritual head of the household and of living a life that will exemplify Christ's lordship without alienating the spiritually weak or apostate spouse.

Equal Partners or Parent and Child?

A second area in which people can face difficulty because they married someone who was not their equal is in the area of emotional stability. Some people will be attracted to someone who is not a psychological equal. Very sensitive souls who think it is their Christian duty to care for someone wounded may marry someone emotionally crippled in childhood because it is a way of ministering to others. As a result, they are locked into a life of parenting as substitute mother or father.

One young woman I talked to recently believed it was her destiny to nurse a psychologically wounded man for the rest of her life. When she went on to talk of her dreams of helping people in the Third World, I challenged her. Either she marries and takes care of that one emotional cripple for life, or like Mother Teresa she could give her life to help many. Of course in the process of realizing this goal, she might meet a husband with the same vision.

Loving the Real Person
A final way in which Christians can go wrong in marriage is to fall in love with an ideal rather than a real person. As Scott Peck has pointed out, the experience of falling in love is basically a mixing of "individual sexual drives and external stimuli which serves to increase the probability of sexual pairing."[4] Unfortunately, the young—or not so young—who fall in love have very little information on the role of their sexual drives. Sincere Christians may, in fact, believe that the experience of falling in love is evidence that God's will is for them to marry.

But they may be marrying an object of their affections who exists only in their minds, not in reality. The real person may be quite different than the one their romantic feelings have led them to imagine. Perhaps this confusion of real and ideal, of God's will and sexual drives, is the reason why so many Christian marriages end in divorce, as did our friend Joe's.

A strapping basketball player from a model Christian home, Joe fell in love with the most glamorous cheerleader on a Christian campus. After starting to date Joe, she made her commitment to Jesus Christ. Was it to please him? We don't know, nor do we know why she agreed to marry him and go with him to the mission field.

That's where we met them: she—immaculately groomed, and as cold, beautiful and bored as a china doll, and he—bubbling over with stories of his exciting ministry. One day, when we saw him alone, he told of the excellent work being done by a single woman assigned to women's work in his mission. While there was nothing questionable about his working relationship with her, it revealed how little he had in common with his wife. It made me wonder why he hadn't chosen someone like this woman—who would share his ministry—when he was shooting baskets back at college. Maybe he thought the cheerleader who had affirmed him on the basketball court would continue to cheer him on the long journey of marriage. But she didn't. She left him.

So what went wrong? Maybe they were trapped into this poor match by falling in love sexually and then continuing—encouraged by the romantic ideals so prevalent on Christian campuses—to live under the illusion that they were meant for each other. The Christian myth about marriage tells us that there is one and only one person for us to marry, and that one person has been picked by God long ago and will be revealed to us through loving feelings. God gets the blame for our poor decisions.

If "falling in love" is the entrance to the fairy-tale world of the prince and princess who live happily forever after, "falling out of love" becomes the sure sign that we have misread the stars—or the will of the Almighty. After that, it's a choice between divorce, or an endurance contest "until death do us part." But we can be sure that if we are married, then it is God's will for us to try to work things out for the better with our spouses.

Learning from Traditional Cultures

Once a couple get married, there are other factors in our society which work against the formation of lifetime bonds. One of these is the lack of support from the extended family. In many non-Western societies, choosing a mate is a family affair. Of course there are obvious limitations to this matchmaking system, but maybe we can also see the advantages. One is that it avoids the pitfalls of our method of choosing a mate by falling in love.

The key to the system is the choice of mates from similar family backgrounds so that the marriage adjustment becomes easier. Traditional societies are not interested in experimenting with a marriage to an individual from an exotic and radically different background. Their practical common sense sees this as an unnecessary strain on the marriage. The Chinese have a proverb that says the best marriages take place between couples who played together as children. This means that the parents were probably friends with similar social and economic standing, and the children probably had many shared interests and were about the same age.

By contrast marriages in the West are often decided strictly by personal preference. Most of us have known men who prefer to marry women who are younger physically and less advanced spiritually, socially and intellectually. On the other side of the coin, we know of women who are looking for men who are older physically and more mature spiritually, intellectually and socially—as an added source of identity for them.

The Problem of Dependency and Control
The bad marriages that result from such wrong initial choices often become relationships of dependency and control. A marriage where one partner is wholly reliant on the other for decisions and direction can frequently be confused with real love. But it is far from it. Long ago Jesus warned his followers of the human desire to control: "You know that those who are supposed to rule over the Gentiles lord it over them, and their great men exercise authority over them. But it shall not be so among you; but whoever would be great among you must be your servant, and whoever would be first among you must be slave of all" (Mk 10:42-44).

In a traditional society where men ruled over women and masters ruled over their slaves, such teaching was revolutionary. It still is—

because we still have marriages of dependency with all their accompanying destructive effects. Men fall into sin by ruling over women, and women retaliate through subtle manipulation.

Such a woman told Scott Peck that she loved her husband so much she couldn't live without him. He answered her: "You are mistaken, you do not love your husband. . . . What you describe is parasitism, not love. When you require another individual for your survival, you are a parasite on that individual. There is no choice, no freedom involved in your relationship. It is a matter of necessity rather than love. Love is the free exercise of choice. Two people love each other only when they are quite capable of living without each other but choose to live with each other."[5]

Peck goes on to name the "passive dependent personality disorder" as the most common of all psychiatric disorders. Such people have no sense of personal identity except in their relationships. Both men and women can be passively dependent, but perhaps it occurs more commonly among women:

> She develops a "phobia" about driving at some point after marriage and stops. The effect . . . is to render her almost totally dependent on her husband and chain her husband to her by her helplessness. . . . Because this behavior usually gratifies the dependency needs of both spouses, it is almost never seen as sick. . . . Through such behavior, passive dependent marriages may be made lasting and secure, but they cannot be considered either healthy or genuinely loving, because the security is purchased at the price of freedom and the relationship serves to retard or destroy the growth of the individual partners. . . . A good marriage can exist only between two strong and independent people.[6]

The desire for this type of marriage often starts with a young woman's dreams of a strong, decisive man: "I want a fellow who can take over and be in charge," said one woman after a date where the man had had a hard time making up his mind. Was she really looking for a man to love and share her life with, or for a father to whom she could abdicate responsibility for the rest of her life? On the husband's side, since decision making is so important in the maturing process for men and women, how can a man say he loves his wife if he stunts her growth in this important area?

But somehow it is on this issue of decision making that many men are most threatened. They have been told that every ship has to have a captain. But my home is not a ship and my husband and I don't constitute a crew that needs any other captain than Jesus Christ. Christ is the Head of the body of believers—the captain of our salvation (Col 2:19; Heb 2:10 KJV).

By the same token, the woman should not be the one to make all the decisions and to "run" the marriage. In these days of women's liberation, we are seeing more marriages where a weak man is married to a strong, aggressive woman. She may have married him because she did not want to be dominated by a macho male, but she ends up being the macho one. And she, too, is ignoring her spouse's need to grow and mature. In the final analysis, God is the only one who can control us without hurting us. And only God can save us from divorce.

The Black Death of Divorce
In the fourteenth century the plague spread over Europe and parts of Asia, killing people in all strata of society. Homes were deserted and closed as maybe only one or two members of the family were left. Life for many in those days ended in weeping.

Today the greatest problem we face in the West is not such an epidemic, and not even the threat of a nuclear explosion, but the weeping that comes from broken relationships. When families disintegrate, our society falls apart. That's why we call divorce the new Black Death that stalks the land and leaves the wounded and dying to fend for themselves, often alienated and alone in the world.

"Sometimes I feel like a motherless child a long way from home," is an old song which will be a song of the future:

At current rates, half of all American marriages begun in the early

1980's will end in divorce. . . . One out of four children is not living with both parents. . . . By the year 2000, three kinds of families will dominate the personal lives of most Americans: Families of first marriages, single-parent families, and families of remarriages. . . . If the current rate of divorce persists, about half of all the children will spend some time in a single-parent family before they reach 18. . . . It will not be uncommon . . . for children born in the 1980's to . . . live with both parents for several years, live with their mothers after their parents divorce, live with their mothers and stepfathers, live alone for a time . . . live with someone of the opposite sex without marrying, get married, get divorced, live alone again, get remarried, and end up living alone once more following the death of their spouses.[7]

We can't read these predictions without being gripped by the sad saga of broken relationships. Children will shuffle back and forth between two sets of parents. Each time the children pass between the former spouses, there is the reminder of a former life that has been destroyed. This is the theme of August Strindberg's drama with the fitting title, *The Link*. Through the children the divorced couple remain linked forever. One of my good friends is tortured each time her former husband drives up to her house with his new wife to pick up the children. Without the children—and her sense of responsibility to keep them in touch with their father—she would not have to face such agony.

Whose fault is it? Why should such a tragedy ever happen? We have already mentioned some of the causes of divorce, such as choosing a mate who is not a spiritual or psychological equal, or falling in love with an ideal rather than a real person. And we have seen how in traditional cultures some of these problems that develop in courtship are avoided through family matchmaking.

Where Other Countries Differ

Part of the problem seems to be that divorce is just too available and is too easily treated as the solution to a bad marriage. Every marriage faces serious problems at times. And this is especially true where the spouses are growing and maturing, perhaps for the first time. One partner may grow distant from the other:

> Any number of things may initiate the growing-up process. The husband may take a sensitivity training program at work. He may begin to realize that he can become a whole person with feelings too. Or he may meet a woman who is a whole person and experience what it means to have a relationship with an adult. . . . The wife may . . . decide to go back to school or get a job. . . . She may meet a man who relates to her as an equal rather than trying to parent her.[8]

Such conflicts are handled differently in non-Western cultures than they are in ours. This may be one reason why divorce is so rare elsewhere. In the Philippines, for example, the extended family on both sides would often come to the aid of a couple in serious conflict. There might be a family council with representatives from both clans to help the partners solve their differences. But in our Western society such kindness is looked on as an invasion of privacy.

Another difference in societies, which might explain the dramatic difference in divorce rates, is that our society is so mobile. In the name of progress moves are made to new localities where there is no extended family. New in town—with a larger salary and the prestige that goes with the promotion—the couple has no private world but each other. Locked into just this narrow relationship, they tend to expect too much of each other, depending on the spouse for friendship, inspiration, recreation, and just plain tender loving care. Dependency leads to a sense of claustrophobia, resulting in one or both of them wanting to bail out.

Even without being in a new situation, couples in the West tend to expect too much of each other. The myth of romantic love tells me that complete understanding and appreciation can be found in a single relationship with one particular person. But common sense should tell me that no other human being can fully meet my deepest needs. My husband can't. Only God can. The same God can also give me the gift of love to forgive my spouse, to laugh at my fickle feelings, and to act in love in opposition to my feelings.

Christian Marriage

As has already been mentioned in passing, one of the earmarks of a strong marriage will be commitment—the decision to act lovingly even when you don't feel like it, even if that lack of loving feelings continues for weeks, months or maybe even years.

But perhaps even more than this raw decision to be committed to each other, a Christian marriage will be characterized by mutual respect and understanding. In Genesis 2 we have the detailed description of the creation of Eve. According to one Bible scholar,

Adam immediately recognized that she was made of the "same stuff" as he, and fulfilled God's design to make a "helper for him." "Fit for him" is defined in the standard Hebrew-English lexicon as meaning "equal and corresponding to." "Helper" in the Old Testament never indicates "subordinate" or "under the authority of." The Hebrew word "ezer" appears 17 times in the Old Testament. Most of the references are to God as our "helper". . . . Where "ezer" is used of someone other than God, the context indicates that the meaning is something like "ally." The . . . description of Eve (here) is "a strength or power or partner equal and corresponding to him."[9]

This passage in Genesis 2:18-25 is one of the most beautiful passages in the Bible. It describes the ideal marital relationship. The two were exactly suited for one another. They were, in the literal sense, "made for each other."

After the fall, when all relationships were broken, God declared that as a result of sin, the woman's desire would be for her husband, and he would rule over her. At the same time, childbirth would become a painful experience and producing food would become tedious. The history of humanity from that point has been, in a sense, an effort to overcome those effects of sin. In childbirth, we use breathing exercises and medication to ease the pain. In agriculture we use tractors and fertilizers to increase the yield, and in marriage we use mutual understanding and God's grace to overcome the sin that seeks to separate us and to allow one person to dominate the other in a destructive manner.

Just as Christ came to take away the effects of sin on our eternal souls, so the grace of God can make all the difference in a marriage. Like Adam and Eve, we will feel naked and ashamed when we know we have sinned against our spouse, and we will try to hide from God and each other. But we must be honest enough to admit that we are in need of reconciliation. A sad note is often heard among those deeply wounded by a spouse. They say they do not feel that there is enough to be gained from reconciliation to make the effort worthwhile. Family relationships are measured in terms of profit and loss, rather than looked on as a gift from a loving and caring God.

My Parents and Me

I learned to say, "I'm sorry, please forgive me," because as a little girl I heard my parents say this to each other. Theirs was the closest to a perfect marriage I have ever seen, not because they were perfect people, but because they were honest enough to admit their weaknesses and to draw on God's unconditional love.

My parents shared the childrearing responsibilities as they shared ministry on the mission field in China. My father treated my mother, not only as a queen, but as an equal, having as much concern and respect for her ministry and schedule as he had for his own. In *Women at the Crossroads* I have gone into more detail on how they worked out their joint ministries.[10]

Looking back, I can now see the natural circumstances that contributed to my putting these wonderful memories on the back burner during my university days. After my father's death and our imprisonment during the war in China, our family had been separated and I had come to the U.S. to go to college. Having come from a very different background, I was often disappointed in the shallow discipleship I found among many Christian students. Hence, when I met a group that took Christ's call to obedience seriously, I became so impressed with them that I did not think critically about all their teachings. They loved the Lord and set about to make disciples of all nations. But there was one flaw: They did not treat men and women as mutual partners in either marriage or ministry.

My mother saw these problems. She had been brought up under the teachings of Hudson Taylor. The China Inland Mission had since 1865 tried to treat men and women as equals on the mission field. At a conference as early as 1888 Hudson Taylor reported that "the C.I.M. had many inland stations manned only by ladies and the assistance of native workers."[11] Through most of its history, two-thirds of the mission was composed of women. This is how the inland provinces of China were evangelized, and I had been an eyewitness to my mother's and father's parts in that ministry.

It was with a heavy heart, then, that my mother watched me join a mission whose theology on women was so different from Hudson Taylor's. I signed a contract to teach English literature at a state university in Asia under the auspices of this mission. There I found myself present in one of those special times in history when the Spirit of God was moving on a group of people. Students who could not discuss Christianity in class because of the rules of the university came to my student center and talked by the hour, responding to Christ's call on their lives.

I was engaged to Bob and scheduled to leave Asia to be married at the end of the year. But I was so sure God wanted me to stay on with these students that I wrote to Bob—and contacted the mission—about his joining me at my post or our postponing marriage for a year. To my surprise the mission responded with a sudden notice from U.S. headquarters that I was to leave at the end of the school year. I was not even allowed to stay to find and train a replacement for the university post and its offshoot—the evangelization that was happening at the student center.

Happy to see Bob, but with a broken heart and mixed-up ideas,

I entered married life. My ministry had been the overflow of my love for Jesus. When that ministry was taken away, the unspoken message was that love for Christ was not a priority for a wife. I didn't feel I knew anymore what it meant to be a Christian wife. Nothing that was happening to me agreed with the training I had received from my parents. Something in me cried out that I was on the wrong path. But I couldn't sort it out till I hit the rock bottom of depression and despair. Though I loved Bob dearly and longed to be close to him as well as close to my heavenly bridegroom, it was hard to put the two together.

Double Marriage

The double vision of combining an earthly marriage with a heavenly union gives us "double happiness"—a famous motif in Chinese culture. There should be no conflict once we see that this is God's plan for us. Instead of inner turmoil between love for God and love for one's spouse, God's intention is harmony.

God graciously sent Bob and me to the Philippines where we saw this integration in the most choice of God's servants. We saw models of marriage where husband and wife both put God first in their lives. In fact, the more the man and woman were focused on Christ, the better they were able to focus also on each other's needs. And the lives of these godly people spilled over into ministry to others.

Our union with Christ will result in ministry whether we plan it or not. The more I am united to Jesus Christ in deep love, the more I will love my husband and children, and the life of caring will reach into a world that needs the love of Jesus.

As we observed these models, Bob and I realized that we needed to work on our marriage to better conform it to God's ideal. I, especially, had to work through many conflicting ideas and feelings. And to complicate matters further, I had to personally learn to die to self in order to love my enemies. The fact that we were both strong personalities did not make it any easier. We were also a mixed marriage: Swedish/American and Norwegian/ Chinese! (We hadn't played together as children.)

It took hours and hours to wade through all the slush that had accumulated. We used our days off on the beach in Davao, our holidays in the mountains of Baguio, and furlough time in Norway. How grateful! I am for a husband willing to take time that should have been for relaxation to work through these problems that were still boiling in my subconscious. God used him to bring healing to my spirit.

And now I thank God for the wonderful marriage and ministry he has given us for most of the thirty-two years we have been together. It is based on the fact that we both need God's grace daily and receive it freely to shower on each other.

And the best is yet to come. For as forgiven sinners, we are the chosen bride of Christ that will be presented before him "in splendor, without spot or wrinkle . . . holy and without blemish" (Eph 5:27). This is the vocabulary of the Bible from the early days of God's call to Israel, through the prophets like Isaiah, Hosea and Malachi, all the way to the last page of Revelation. The marriage on earth that has been at the core of human existence since Adam and Eve is but a shadow of the marriage to take place when we reach our Home. The two covenants involved in the double relationship are different and yet strangely similar, for both are based on unconditional love—God's willingness to die for us and our willingness to die for Jesus Christ, and for each other as husband and wife.

This is the dynamic truth my parents passed on to me as they modeled marriage for me. And this is also the truth Bob and I have tried to pass on to our children. How happy I was a few years ago when my daughter Kirsten and her husband, Paul, chose the theme of the marriage in heaven for their outdoor wedding ceremony. As the father of the bride read and reflected on the texts they had chosen, we were all captured by the message of the marriage to come, and we were enveloped by the magnificent sunset over Lake Valentine and the festive mood of the moment. What more could I ask in life? I had reached a mountain peak. My firstborn child and her husband were telling the world that their covenant of love was but a picture of the real marriage that lies ahead of us all at the end of our pilgrimage—the great Marriage of the Lamb that will consummate our love relationship with our Savior:

Let us rejoice and exult and give him the glory, for the marriage of the Lamb has come, and his Bride has made herself ready; . . . Then I saw a new heaven and a new earth; . . . And I saw the holy city, new Jerusalem, coming down out of heaven from God, prepared as a bride adorned for her husband; and I heard a loud voice from the throne saying, "Behold, the dwelling of God is with men. He will dwell with them, and they shall be his people." (Rev 19:7; 21:1-3)

3

SLOWING US DOWN: SEX, POWER AND MONEY

J EREMIAH HAS BEEN CALLED THE WEEP-
ing prophet because he weeps over people who have lost direction
in life. They "stumble in their paths, the ancient ways, and they take
to byways and unmade roads" (Jer 18:15 NEB). Jeremiah was chosen by God to call such people back to their first love for God.

We need some weeping prophets today to call people back—with
the broken heart of a Jeremiah—to the ancient paths of loving God
and their families. Love is the highest value in life (1 Cor 13:13),
and has to be worked out, not in isolation or alienation but in
community with God and others, including the family.

Many Christians today have strayed from truly Christian values,
and their lives suffer from inconsistency and the pain of broken
relationships and unkept promises. R. C. Sproul has seen the problem: "How can 60 million born-again people, who have been

trained and nurtured to be light to a dying world have no demonstrable impact on the culture?"[1]

The reason is that they have forsaken the ancient Christian values and adopted the values of society. Until we go back to truly biblical ways of thinking we will be overwhelmed by the power and influence of our culture. We must repent of our twentieth-century me-centeredness and ask God's forgiveness for having left him as our first love and gone after other lovers.

But specifically what are the other values that keep us from loving our God, and in turn loving our family and others? In what concrete areas do we need to repent so that the barriers to family unity will be removed?

Sex, Money and Power

John, the apostle of love, alluded to these three areas of sex, power and money when, in the tradition of Jeremiah, he called Christians to repentance hundreds of years later: "Do not love the world or the things in the world. If any one loves the world, love for the Father is not in him. For all that is in the world, the lust of the flesh and the lust of the eyes and the pride of life, is not of the Father but is of the world" (1 Jn 2:15-16).

As John made this statement about the values of the world that keep us from intimacy with God, he might have had in mind both the temptation in the Garden of Eden and the temptation of Jesus in the wilderness. Both situations illustrated what John calls "the lust of the flesh"—the temptation to let the physical desire for food or sex overpower us.

"The lust of the eyes" was also present—coveting what our eyes see and wanting it at any cost, including disobedience to God, homage to the evil one, or imprisonment in a quest for money to get it. And "the pride of life" was very much in evidence, too, in both temptations—the desire for power over others and the pride which comes with achieving power and thus being like God (Gen 3:1-7; Mt 4:1-11).

From Jesus, John and the other disciples learned how crucial these three areas are for every human being. The disciples must have seen Jesus' heartache over families where fathers looked beyond the marriage union for sexual satisfaction; where parents loved their possessions more than each other; and where spouses put achievement—reaching a place of power—above family relationships.

I have read that Billy Graham in his ministry has taken special care to avoid these three temptations. He prays for extra protection against wrong involvement with women, love of money, and pride. He has seen the power these things have to destroy the ministry of successful preachers.[2]

Richard Foster has also spoken and written at length about these three temptations in his book *Money, Sex and Power*. God's Word makes it clear that these temptations are the primary ones which will affect the lives of individuals, families and even whole societies.[3]

We not only see these themes in Jesus' temptation in the wilderness, but Matthew 19 and Mark 10 give us a unique account of what looks like one day in Jesus' life when he discussed sex, power and money. It's like a three-act play with first the Pharisees, then a group of mothers, and finally the rich young ruler.

The Barrier of Sex

The Pharisees asked about family life—whether divorce was lawful (Mt 19:1-12, Mk 10:1-12). Jesus used the opportunity to teach them about the sanctity of both the married and the single life. He reminded them that the sexual union was to take place only within the bonds of marriage, elaborating that "a man shall leave his father and mother and be joined to his wife, and the two shall become one flesh. . . . What therefore God has joined together, let not man put asunder."

The words of Jesus must have sounded like music in the ears of the women who were listening. They had left their parents and hometowns to join their husbands' families. While the Old Testament laws did not show contempt for women, by Jesus' time rabbinic tradition had lowered their status. Men were persons and women were property. Therefore, men could divorce their wives if they found another woman more beautiful.[4]

When the Pharisees reminded Jesus that even Moses allowed divorce, Jesus replied, "For your hardness of heart Moses allowed you to divorce your wives, but from the beginning it was not so. And I say to you: whoever divorces his wife, except for unchastity, and marries another, commits adultery" (Mt 19:8-9). Jesus was putting an end to the double standard by appealing to the creation narrative.

At this point even the disciples balked at Jesus' standards: "If such is the case of a man with his wife, it is not expedient to marry." Jesus answered by giving the alternative of singleness. He told of eunuchs who are that way from birth, others who have been made eunuchs by society and a third group who "have made themselves eunuchs for the sake of the kingdom of heaven" (Mt 19:10-12).

In contrast to the world's endless possibilities of sexual unions, Jesus offered only these two alternatives. We can be faithful to our marriage partners, or as the Catholic and Protestant orders have done through the ages, we can take the vow of chastity for the sake of the kingdom. This has been common in the modern missionary movement where thousands of single people, mostly women, have invaded pagan cultures for Christ.

"But what do I do about my sex drives?" a single woman friend asked. What people through the ages have done. Single men and women have loved God and challenged the god of sex not to run their lives. Whether married or single our sex drives are under the control of God who made us as sexual beings. Both alternatives demand chastity—the married person has sex with only one, and the unmarried with none!

Before divorce was an accepted alternative, people took the decision to marry very seriously. And if they made a mistake, they made the best of it. As a result, there are many old stories about the impossible spouse—humor built around the recognition that marriage was for life. The Norwegian fairy tale called "The Hare Who Had Been Married" is an example of such humor:

There was once a Hare who went for a walk in the green field. "Hop and skip and jump ahigh," sang the Hare in great glee . . . and then stood up on his hind legs and looked around and listened. Then came a Fox sneaking across the field.

"Good day, good day," said the Hare. "I'm so happy today for having been married. . . . I must tell you about it."

"That must have been very nice," said the Fox.

"Well, it wasn't always so nice either, for she was pretty tough at times too. A real devil she could be, the one I got for a wife," said the Hare.

"It must have been . . . bad for you then," said the Fox.

"Oh, but it wasn't altogether . . . bad. . . . I got a good dowry with her, for she had a house," said the Hare.

"But that was a fine thing to get," said the Fox.

"Well, that wasn't so good either, for the house burnt down," said the Hare. And everything . . . went up in flames."

"Oh, but that really was too bad!" said the Fox.

"No, it wasn't too bad after all, for she burnt up with it," said the Hare.[5]

The Barrier of Power

As Jesus was concluding his remarks on chastity, a group of mothers interrupted him (Mt 19:13-15; Mk 10:13-16). The women had come with their children in tow. Sensing Jesus' kinship with the powerless, they had confidence to approach him as powerless women to ask for a special blessing for their powerless children.

Immediately, the disciples tried to chase the children away. As Jesus' disciples they believed they had the authority to shield him from unimportant people. But Jesus moved as quickly as the disciples did. Shifting his teaching from the lust for sex to the lust for power, he used strong words to make it clear that powerless children—like all disenfranchised people—had a special place in his schedule and in his heart. In fact, he said that the children belonged to the kingdom of heaven.

Jesus' words must have shocked the Jews. We are all part of a pecking order, and we tend to look for someone we can lord it over. But Jesus said that it was not to be that way with those who choose to follow him: "Whoever would be great among you must be your servant, and whoever would be first among you must be slave of all" (Mk 10:43-44).

Jesus himself took a towel and washed the disciples' feet to model this principle for us. But instead of following in his footsteps, we have confused the Christian message by bringing the power struggle of the world into the sanctuaries of the church and the Christian home.

But all through the centuries there have also been devout believers who have turned their backs on power. In the monasteries and convents of the Middle Ages, the vow of obedience cut across a person's natural desire for power. And thousands of modern missionaries like my parents have served a lifetime in obscure regions of the world "mean, unnoted and unknown," as the saying then went.[6]

In millions of Christian homes, too, mothers and fathers have laid down their lives for each other and for their children, shunning the quest for power both inside and outside the home. I think of the many beautiful Christians I met in the Philippines in the squatter huts or the tiny nipa cottages of tenant farmers, whose lives pivoted around the survival of their immediate and extended families. Sacrificial love bound these strong families together.

By contrast, those who worship power destroy their homes and their families. Battered wives and children are a common topic of conversation today as the cruelty of authoritarian men is being exposed in American society. Equally damaging is the movement that demands that women become the powerful ones in our society. Caught in the war between power-hungry parents are children who are wounded for life. Jesus warns us that it is better to "be drowned in the depth of the sea" than to cause "one of these little ones who believe in me to sin" (Mt 18:6).

The Barrier of Money

As Jesus finished blessing the powerless children that memorable day, the rich young ruler showed up (Mt 19:16-30; Mk 10:17-31). His wealth became the crucial issue that day as Jesus told him to sell all that he had and give it to the poor. He was called by the Savior of the world to radical discipleship. He could enter a right relationship with his God by giving up his god of money. But the man refused Jesus' generous offer and left sorrowfully: "It is easier for a camel to go through the eye of a needle than for a rich man to enter the kingdom of God," Jesus told his astonished disciples.

"Who then can be saved?" they asked in exasperation.

Jesus used the opportunity to show that what looks impossible to our earthly value system is still possible with God. He knew that his disciples, except for Judas, would follow him and in some cases die as martyrs, even though they were promised no salary. Looking ahead, he also knew that many of his future followers would go to the desert and listen to God—away from the noise of the world—and from this group would grow the missionary orders for men and women. These disciples would take vows of "chastity, poverty and obedience," thus challenging the worldly values of sex, money and power.

The church in Laodicea, one of the wealthiest industrial centers in the Roman Empire, also faced this choice between the god of mammon and the God of the universe. Laodicea was known for its production of fine black wool and Phrygian powder used in treating eye diseases, along with its hot mineral springs. Proud of their wealth, the citizens had refused all help from Rome when the city was wiped out by an earthquake in A.D. 60.[7] It was not too long after they rebuilt their city that John wrote to them: "You say, I am rich, I have prospered, and I need nothing; not knowing that you are wretched, pitiable, poor, blind, and naked" (Rev 3:17).

Everything was turned upside down. Rich Laodiceans were told they were poor, specialists in eye medicine were told they were blind, and people dressed in 100 per cent lamb's wool were told they were naked! John goes on to tell them to buy "gold refined by fire, that you may be rich, and white garments to clothe you . . . and salve to anoint your eyes, that you may see" (Rev 3:18). The gold tried in the fire is faith, the garment is the robe of righteousness, and the salve is the Holy Spirit to anoint the eyes to see spiritual truth.

John, speaking for Jesus, goes on to say to the Laodicean Christians: "Behold, I stand at the door and knock; if any one hears my voice and opens the door, I will come in to him and eat with him, and he with me" (Rev 3:20). Today we in the West are the wealthy Christians—all well-dressed, whose every pain is taken care of by miracle drugs. But haven't we like the Laodiceans left Jesus standing on the outside of our busy and cluttered lives, knocking?

This makes us wonder what Jesus would have said to the Yuppies of the 1980s. "They live to buy," says the *Newsweek* caption: "Affluent, acquisitive and influential, Yuppies are becoming the prize segment of the national market. . . . What enhances the importance of being Yuppie is that they sit on top of the largest, richest, best-educated generation ever born."[8]

The Cost of Affluence

Someone is taking the punishment for our society's emphasis on money, sex and power. And I believe it's the children. The curse of industry and the progress it has brought has been to take first the father and then the mother out of the home. Among people who see the problem, there's often a lot of blaming of the other parent. Men have told me that their wives insisted on working and taking the children to day-care. The fathers sound so helpless—as if there's not a thing they could do about it. I can imagine them standing before God, like Adam of old, and saying, "You see, Lord, Eve was a feminist. That's why my kids didn't get the parenting they needed."

In such families, both parents may have demanding jobs with prestigious firms because the family needs two salaries to maintain their affluent lifestyle. And the high price of affluence is paid by powerless children. The saddest part of it all is that so many parents think they have no choice. Many of them dislike the work they do and tell me they would love to be home, but they feel trapped. How will they pay the bills?

There is nothing immoral about working. In fact, there is something very creative about using all the talents God has given us. What is immoral is to ignore the spiritual and emotional needs of our children, especially during their most impressionable years. In the early years of a child's life the child needs a parent or good parent substitute to give him or her a sense of security as well as Christian training.

But there are other alternatives. There are people who are going against this tide. Our good friend, Dr. Jim Sheard, wanted to see more of his twin boys. He had a job as an industrial psychologist with a prestigious firm in a metropolitan area. By moving to a job in a small town, he took a big cut in salary, fringe benefits, pension and status. But he is much more content with his new smaller company. He has little chance of promotion or salary increases, but his hours are shorter and more regular, giving him more time to spend with his family.

Jim and Maureen returned after ten months to report to the small group that had helped them pray through to this decision. They were so grateful for their new and slower pace of life because it has given them more time for God and family, as well as new and unexpected ways of ministering to needy people around them.

I have also heard women blame their husbands for bad conditions in the home. "He won't take any responsibility for the kids," some say. "So why should I? Why should the woman always be the one that's blamed for emotionally wounded children?"

My brother and sister-in-law faced the problem of who should work and who should parent the children. And they came up with an unusual solution:

> We found that when we were both working full time, our lives
> became incredibly complicated, and our expenses and standard
> of living quickly expanded to a point where we felt just as
> strapped as we would have on one income. And there were the
> kids. They had a pediatrician for a mother who preferred, if at all
> possible, that preschoolers like they should receive their primary
> care from one of us, not from surrogates. And their father agreed.
> So one of us would have to continue subordinating a career to
> the obligations of a home. . . . I [the father] was ready for some-
> thing new . . . having a daddy concentrating on the home while
> mama pursued her career and brought in the mortgage and groc-
> ery money. . . . Since my career had dominated the first decade
> of our marriage, we would now trade roles.[9]

Of course, many women do not yet have enough background and
training to allow them to take over full responsibility for breadwin-
ning. The point of the story is not to advocate role changes for the
sake of role changes—or to appease feminists! But while I doubt if
God is really concerned about who brings in the mortgage and
grocery money, I believe the Almighty has given us some strong
guidance about the training of our children.

"But don't you think the children are a woman's main responsibility in life?" I was asked by someone who was skeptical of my
commitment to the family.

Of course children are a mother's main responsibility. But I want
to go farther than that. For *both* the mother and the father the
children are the first responsibility in life. They are not just the
responsibility of the mother.

In my generation, most mothers stayed home, but many children
were adversely affected by the lack of an attentive father. He thought
his job was finished when he brought home the pay check. So why
should we return to the "good old days" that weren't so good? Why
not return to the biblical mandate of both parents being responsible
for their children's upbringing and Christian formation?

We need mothers and fathers who will make time for their children, first, by trying to live on one income during the preschool years. After that, the crucial time is the morning before school and the afternoon when the children return home. Pressure needs to be put on big business to be more humane in their policies, allowing some parents to come late to work (after the kids are safely on the bus), and others to leave early to be home when the children are. If the marketplace would cooperate with family life, we could eliminate the "latchkey kid" from our society.

One expert estimates that there are 10 million latchkey kids in the United States—almost a quarter of the school population. In an article entitled, "Teach Your Kids What to Do When You Are Not Home," the writer suggests, "Never tell anyone on the telephone that you are home alone. Say, 'My Mom can't come to the phone right now. Can I take a message?' (It may be a good idea to have your child practice until he or she becomes comfortable with telling 'white lies')."[10] The problem is very real. Children must not let strangers know they are in the house alone. But is lying the solution?

Robert Vernon, a police officer from Los Angeles, has had plenty of experience with "latchkey kids." He mourns the situation:

Neither mother nor father is there to welcome the children home from school, to give them the guidance, encouragement, and love that is needed during the formative years. . . . We have a standard of living that is unequalled. . . . Often, however, neglected children—little ones who feel insecure and rejected—are the ones who pay the price for our "good life." Whether consciously or not, many parents have come to value material success over and above human values. . . . Things have been given precedence over the most precious possessions we have—our children. But spurned love often turns into hostility and hatred. The Bible says, "Fathers, do not provoke your children to anger" (Eph 6:4). I believe the most profound way we provoke our children is through rejection. Our epidemic of rebellious children is a direct result of neglect, or when material gain replaces guidance and love.[11]

If parents are not willing to put children ahead of outside interests, what other options are open? The obvious one for those who want two careers—with no interruptions for childrearing—is just not to have children.

For a Christian couple this can be a selfish cop-out unless they are motivated by a sense of call to use their two careers to help people in a hurting world. Maybe they want to obey Micah 6:8—"What does the Lord require of you but to do justice, and to love kindness, and to walk humbly with your God?" For a couple with this as their motive, a child-free marriage is not immoral. But there is something immoral about bringing children into the world who will feel rejected—left to fend for themselves.

Children Need Models

A love for money and the affluent lifestyle it buys can separate us from God and our families. It can also keep us from becoming models of Christian love for our children. For example, when we are rich, we will find it difficult to show concern for the poor and powerless.

News articles report that the gap is widening in the U.S. between the rich and the poor.[12] As the money gap gets wider, so does the communications gap. As couples increase their standards of living they tend to move out of working-class neighborhoods into more affluent communities. They no longer see bag ladies hanging around outside the grocery store, and they lose touch with the neighbor whose health problems kept him from putting adequate food on the table for his family. After the move, they change churches, too, to match the new neighborhood, so they seldom have to face people in church who have lost their jobs and are in danger of losing their homes.

"But how can we give to the poor when we are barely able to pay our bills?" they might ask. But they forget that their house payment has doubled since they moved. If they'd stayed in the old neighborhood they would've been able to give more money away.

I learned to care for the poor as I grew up in China and later as I brought up my own children in the Philippines. In the Philippines I learned to laugh about life with people who were too poor to do much else. And when the corruption of the Marcos regime was exposed, I laughed with them again. Filipinos, always ready for a bit of humor, advertised The Imelda Doll. The ad read: She "comes complete with 3000 pairs of shoes, hundreds of designer dresses, 500 black brassieres, dozens of gucci handbags, jewelry, perfume, stocks, bonds, New York office buildings and one deposed dictator."[13]

In a country where eighty per cent or more live below the poverty line, Imelda's lifestyle was hardly consistent with that of John the Baptist who preached, "He who has two coats, let him share with him who has none" (Lk 3:11). But also in poverty-stricken Asia I have known women in worn-out clothes with the joy of heaven on their faces. They are great in the kingdom of heaven. To them has been given the faith to trust God for their needs, and they have been models for me and my children.

What these women gave to their children is the greatest inheritance any of us can give to our sons and daughters—that God is a good God who will take care of our needs. This does not mean that God will take care of all our *wants*. That's where the prosperity doctrine—with nothing but the best for the "king's kids"—has led many moderns astray.

Jesus contrasted the attitudes of the world with those of the kingdom: "Do not be anxious, saying, 'What shall we eat?' or 'What shall we drink?' or 'What shall we wear?' For the Gentiles seek all these things; and your heavenly Father knows that you need them all. But seek first his kingdom and his righteousness, and all these things shall be yours as well" (Mt 6:31-33).

How much we are like a dog—reluctant to drop the three dry bones of sex, power and money, while Jesus stands beside us offering us a feast that is beyond our wildest imagination. God is not an old miser, asking us to give up something without giving us something else a hundred times better in return. When Jesus finished his discourse in Matthew 19, he told the crowds that anyone who left houses or families or lands to follow him would receive a hundredfold in return.

As missionary children in China we were often reminded of the hundredfold in this life, which referred to a quality of life that money could not buy. My mother loved to tell anyone who would listen how good God had been to her and her family through the years. And we can all be sure that God will be good to us if we put him first in our family life, if we sacrifice in order to build the kind of family God wants us to have. We can be assured that God will honor that sacrifice by giving us treasures that are too precious for money.

4

PUTTING
CHRIST
IN THE LEAD

I REMEMBER A SCENE IN NORWAY ON one of those magnificent, sunlit summer days that never seem to end. The family was gathered on a rocky island out in the sea beyond Kristiansand. We were home on furlough from China, and my mother's sister and brother and their families, along with Mormor (mother's mother), the matriarch of the clan, were with us.

My brother Torje was still at the age of innocence when proper swimming attire is not expected in Norway. He enjoyed the long day of swimming, eating and "kosing" (being cozy with others) in the nude, until finally it was time to go home and Mother called him to come and get dressed. Outraged by such a suggestion, he exclaimed, "I can't get dressed in front of all these girls!" At five, his libertinism had some limits. He did have a sense of modesty. Where did he learn it?

I remember another time in the Philippines. We had newly arrived, and our three-year-old Kirsten was eager to show hospitality to a new-found Filipino friend. It was late when Isabel was ready to go home after a lovely evening together. We urged her to spend the night with us, but she hesitated. Anxious to put her at ease and meet all her needs, Kirsten offered: "You know you can use my mother's toothbrush." Where had she learned such hospitality?

Whatever children learn, good or bad, about how to conduct their lives, they learn in the home. Children may be influenced positively or negatively in church or school, but they are molded at home. They are truly the most homemade products in the world.

At some points in Western history the stability present in society as a whole may have made up for shortcomings in individual families. Children from homes that did not nurture them or give them standards to live by sometimes could find those standards taught in the homes of other family members or neighbors. Joey, whose mother is an alcoholic, could find security and a glass of milk after school in a number of homes on his block.

But Americans have always been fascinated by mobility, and now more than ever. So, friendly neighbors and nearby grandparents do not supply the kind of stability they may once have done. Grandma has moved to Florida, and neighbors move so often that we hardly know who is living next door. Add to this mobility the fact that there is no longer a broad consensus about values in our pluralistic society, and you have a mandate for problems at home.

Malcolm Muggeridge was asked in an interview,

"You said [previously] that Western Civilization was going to collapse in less than twenty years. That was an exaggeration, right?"

"Western Civilization has collapsed," answered Muggeridge.

"We must have been out of town. When was that?"

"Since the beginning of the Second World War, Western Society has experienced a complete abandonment of its mores; a complete abandonment of its sense of good and evil. . . . The true crisis of our time has nothing to do with monetary troubles, unemployment, or nuclear weapons. The true crisis has to do with the fact that Western man has lost his way."[1]

Too many of us missed the collapse. Perhaps that's why we don't take our parenting seriously. We don't realize that the full responsibility lies with us to impart to our children the message of love and hope that Jesus came to bring. If they don't hear the good news at home, they may not hear it anywhere else.

But because many parents feel spiritually inadequate for the task, they prefer to hire others to Christianize their children for them. "I went to work so that I could send my children to a Christian school," one mother confided. She was sure that a religious institution would counteract the evils of our society more effectively than she could. When the Christian school didn't produce the desired result, she wondered what had gone wrong.

Other parents church hop, searching for the place that will give their children the best possible Christian training. They get on boards to build bigger and better Christian education facilities and sit on committees to hire the best youth directors the Christian world can offer. The more sophisticated the program, the higher hopes they have that their children will follow Christ.

But then they may become disillusioned about the message being taught in the youth groups and Sunday school. Explaining to me why they were changing churches again, one mother said, "We were just not being fed at First Church."

What does she mean by not being fed? Would we come to church for one big Sunday dinner each week, and then go home and say, "Now I don't have to cook for the rest of the week"? Don't we realize that feeding the family spiritually as well as physically has to take place several times a day, not just once or twice a week?

Parents as Religious Educators
If bringing the family to church is important, bringing the message of the church into the family is even more important. It's in the

home, not the church or Christian school, where spiritual formation takes place. According to one authority:

> Like it or not, parents are religious educators. . . . They continually communicate religious and moral values in what they say and do. So the question then becomes, not whether parents should be involved in their child's faith formation, but how effective they will be in that role. . . . Parents [must] live the basic themes of the gospel, including those of love, forgiveness, compassion, peacemaking, sensitivity.[2]

While becoming models of discipleship for our children is most important, they also need planned instruction in the Christian faith. This serves two purposes: the older generation is renewed and encouraged as they review the great truths of their heritage, while the younger generation is exposed to the dynamic beliefs that have changed lives.

In Deuteronomy 6 we find some principles to guide us in teaching our children. These words were given to God's chosen people as they journeyed from Egypt to the Promised Land. After they reached their destination, they continued to practice these principles:

> You shall love the LORD your God with all your heart, and with all your soul, and with all your might. And these words which I command you this day shall be upon your heart; and you shall teach them diligently to your children, and shall talk of them when you sit in your house, and when you walk by the way, and when you lie down, and when you rise. . . . And you shall write them on the doorposts of your house and on your gates. . . . When your son asks you in time to come, "What is the meaning of the . . . ordinances which the LORD our God has commanded you?" then you shall say to your son, "We were Pharaoh's slaves in Egypt; and the LORD brought us out of Egypt with a mighty hand; and the LORD showed signs and wonders, great and grievous." (Deut 6:4-7, 9, 20-22)

Christians today also have a Promised Land to tell our children about. In so doing we can follow the practical suggestions given in this Deuteronomy passage. There are four different settings suggested here for imparting the word of God in the home:

First, we are to talk naturally about God—the unseen guest at every meal, the silent listener to every conversation—when we sit in the house. But what about the family that is always on the go, rushing from one job and appointment to another, so that they never sit in the house together? They have a sitting room where they never sit, a family room where the family never gathers.

I shall never forget a time in the Philippines when we found ourselves in that trap and had to take action. Both of us cancelled commitments in all directions till we were once more sitting in our house together as a family. Since we were both involved in the business of the kingdom it was easy for us to rationalize that our busyness was justified. But we had to face the fact that God's work beyond the home had to harmonize with God's work in the home— our children.

At other times, we found ourselves in the house together but not communicating because of ill feelings. I am grateful that we usually dealt with these feelings before they became deep hurts. Sometimes our children had a "wounded spirit" and wanted to lock themselves in their rooms. Those were again times when we needed to confess our sins to one another and pray for one another that we might be healed (Jas 5:16). The heat of battle proved sometimes to be the ideal moment to dig into the Bible to see what God had to say about our minor crises.

Deuteronomy 6 also says that we are to talk about God's Word to our children when we walk by the way. When our daughters were small, we often took them for walks and discussed the wonders of God's creation as we came upon a field of wild flowers or watched a sunset together. In a civilization where walking is not often practiced, perhaps we can suggest talking about God while driving.

The third situation where we are to talk about God's Word to our children is when we are going to bed. What a heritage children in

Christian homes have who have learned to end the day with a story from the Bible and prayer. My heart has ached when I have been in homes where children just get a hug and a kiss. We rob ourselves and our children when we miss this opportunity to share together a quiet time with God. Our children used to feel important when we would leave our guests in the living room to sit by their beds and go through the usual ritual. At other times, the company joined in the bedtime story and benefited from their childish insights into God's Word.

The fourth time we are to talk about God's Word to our children is when we rise up. I have spoken with scores of women about the importance of starting the day together at breakfast with Bible reading and prayer. But many respond, "We never eat breakfast together at our house." The problems are real: some have jobs and leave early, others want to sleep in after late hours, and some are always on diets. How can they get together?

A famous Chinese evangelist, Leland Wang, had the motto: "No Bible, no breakfast." This needs to be changed for the American scene to read: "Come for the Bible reading. You may skip the breakfast." Starting out the morning together—if you possibly can—with a sense of God's presence will make a big difference in your family's life. And yet, since God is always present, we cannot single out the morning time as the most sacred. Couples these days need to be very creative about how (and at what time of day) the family can join together for study, discussion and prayer.

But what about the woman who does not get the support of her husband in talking to the children about God's Word? Some of these wait patiently for the father to initiate family devotions. "Doesn't the Bible say that the man is the head of the house?" an attractive mother of five asked me.

"But what if your husband were a drunkard and did not bring home the money you needed for groceries," I asked. "Would you let your kids starve, or would you go out and get a job so you could buy food for them?"

The same law of survival that operates in the physical world must operate in the spiritual realm if we are going to bring up Christian children. The Word of God is our daily bread, and our children will starve without it (Mt 4:4). I suggested to my friend that she place the Bible on the breakfast table along with the toast and juice and coffee: "Let the family know that Bible reading is just part of the breakfast menu."

"But my husband will make fun of me if I just start reading," my friend protested. He might, if he doesn't respect your ideas and values. But if you have a supportive marriage, and if you communicate well with each other, then he should be able to accept this new desire of yours even if he doesn't agree. If he's resistant because of his own religious views, then tell him he doesn't have to listen, so long as the children are allowed to. If he is still resistant, then perhaps there is some other problem—one related to the marriage itself—that's intervening. Maybe you need to try to get at the root of the issues and strengthen the whole marriage in the process.

Some men consider religion to be a "woman's thing." That's why so many churches are full of married women bringing their children but not their husbands. Try to make it clear that religion *is* something in which he can take leadership if he wants to. Let him know you and the kids would appreciate it.

"Faith is the assurance of things hoped for, the conviction of things not seen," we read in Hebrews 11:1. Women need to soak such situations in prayer, knowing that God will honor their faithfulness. "Instead of nagging, use prayer." This is the best advice we can give mothers who walk alone as priests in their homes.

Beyond Teaching to Living

Of course, there are no guarantees in child rearing. Not giving a child Christian training makes it unlikely that he or she will grow up with faith. But they may yet be caught by God along the way. Likewise, Christian training does not guarantee that the child will become a devoutly Christian adult. As John White so aptly points out in *Parents in Pain,* children have free wills, and they may choose a lifestyle that greatly contradicts their parents' views.[3]

Some of these children, however, may have been brought up on a Christianity substitute. Perhaps the real emphasis was on church activities rather than on the lordship of Christ. Or maybe the parents talked very piously but did not live that way. Some hypocrisy is inevitable because all parents are sinners. But children are sensitive to such inconsistency, and they are quick to see if their parents' lives belie their words.

As a test of my own consistency (as well as my memory!) I asked my daughter O-i to describe our home life and how well or poorly the faith was lived out there. I think the wisdom expressed here is as much her own as ours. She has grown rich in knowledge and understanding in recent years. These were her unpremeditated remarks that poured out as we sat on the sofa together after a Sunday dinner with me writing down as much as I could of what she said.

"You had two keys to transferring the value system of your faith to us," she started. "First, you and Pa were both committed to the quest of seeking truth and doing what God wanted us to do. It was a quest beyond tradition, beyond cultural expectations, beyond fulfilling other's expectations of us, or making ourselves respectable. Everything we did was subservient to that. As kids we could sense fakeness.

"Honesty is the second thing I remember. You know, you always fought in front of us kids. You would try to outline all the questions and issues with us—how to relate to Filipinos—how you should relate as husband and wife—how to relate to your work—making cultural adjustments—and theological adjustments—the charismatic movement, the Presbyterian church, the church in the Philippines, social action—you worked it all out in front of us.

"That gave us a realistic picture of what marriage and the church were all about. We saw how Christians should work out their problems. We saw your vulnerability and it served as a model—a good one now as Ross [her husband] and I find that there is a lot that has to be worked through. But we are committed to the goal of reconciliation. Now we are on our own quest and we have to learn to be honest."

She went on to talk of our daily family devotions and the way we often discussed—especially on Saturdays and on vacations when we had more time—how the Bible reading related to life. Our religious rituals therefore had real meaning and direct impact. She also remembers us discussing our wealth in relationship to the poverty around us in the Philippines.

"In life you modeled what you valued and did not value. By not talking about clothes, for instance, you showed they were not important to you. They were a non-issue. You didn't fuss about the length of our miniskirts or if we went braless (which was the fashion). You were not legalistic about those things. Your focus was not on clothes, either in buying or not buying them, while the legalists made clothes seem awfully important."

She went on to tell me how shocked she now is when she realizes what income we lived on. "We had the mentality that money was available if we needed it. Our lifestyle was cheap because our values were on good books, travel and having interesting people at our dinner table. We had a good life—not defined by the TV or movies. You know poverty is partly a state of mind. It was our attitude to wealth that made the difference. Clothes were not a value so as kids we didn't worry about it.

"The family played a stronger role in defining my values than my peers did. I always felt you and Pa understood me best. We lived in three worlds: the Philippines, Norway and the U.S. Only you could understand that. It was only when I got to college that my friends became important to me. You and Pa set my values earlier.

"There wasn't any huge generation gap because you were not preachy and pious, but always struggling to understand what Christianity meant. We had a sense of camaraderie. You were always open to question, attack, discussion, argumentation and negotiation. Kirsten and I didn't have to go outside to raise questions. We were careful and cautious outside, but in the home we could be vulnerable. Because I could air my doubts at home, my faith is now unshakable.

"Some friends in college had faith in a form of Christianity, and when they lost faith in the form, there was no faith left. But we had already demythologized all the forms at home—the Evangelicals, the conservatives, the Fundamentalists, the Episcopalians, the Presbyterians, the Lutherans, the Catholics and all the rest—all forms had been pushed to the end. What was left was the big question: Who is God and how does God speak to us? The key is not to lose sight of the essence—the quest. Others lost their faith because they had no ability to criticize self or to self-reflect. Or their models were not sincere. Kids smell it when the upholders of religion are not authentic.

"Neither materialism nor Christian simplicity can be a goal in life. But if life is oriented around a quest, then the material things of life lose their significance. Too many things like the plight of the Filipino political prisoners were far more important than miniskirts or how much we spent on clothes. And because our values were set early in life, the material things were not important later.

"We were taught a few principles that applied to many circumstances. We were taught about God's grace, and then we were taught to respond to grace by loving God and others—just the two commandments. We did not get caught up in legalisms. We couldn't have many rules because the rules had to change depending on whether we were in the Philippines, Norway, or the U.S.

"As children who lived in many different cultures, we had to adapt a lot. But we did not feel insecure because the emphasis was on the quest for faith. We survived and had a stable home because in the changing circumstances we emphasized the principles. There was a consistency in life even though we moved around.

"Yet while there was consistency, our faith never became stagnant. Rather, it was modeled as something that was vital to you and Pa. And it was maintained through regular times with God. From the moment I could read you thrust devotional books into my hands. Now I know I need my quiet time with God, I need to pray with Ross, and I need to go to church and fellowship with others. These are vessels that cultivate the spark of faith. And that spark was cultivated with truth.

"It's natural for children to become disillusioned when they discover that their parents—or their pastor or other Christians—are fallible. For some kids that can be traumatic, but I don't think it was for us. You always told us the truth about yourself, your mission and your church. We knew about the problem of evil early, so evil was never a shock to us. You continued to work as corrupt people with corrupt people in a corrupt church. And I knew early that I was evil too. That's a powerful theological truth. With it came an emphasis on God's grace breaking through the evil. That's why I am a Christian today.

"Parents need to appreciate spirituality in different forms," O-i continued. "Kirsten and I have adopted different forms of Christianity because we have different natures. But you have been tolerant of the different forms. You weren't upset when I preferred the more formal service of the Episcopalians, nor when Kirsten went to another church for a while. You were able to see beyond the trappings, perhaps because of your cross-cultural experience. Lots of parents have trouble doing that.

"Only as you and Pa were honest about the forms and foibles of Christian institutions did we get to the essence of our faith. After all, if the church is perfect, we don't need Christ.

"When I went away to college I was very grateful for my background. Perhaps because we had been on the mission field, we were like a Malcolm club rather than like parents and children. We had been involved in your work, your problems, and all the people you worked with. You were too busy to worry about how our rooms were decorated or what we wore. Instead, at a young age I was involved in a lot of issues with other people and bigger concerns, not teen-age rebellions. What you were doing was far more interesting to me than what my friends were doing. We faced ethical questions at a young age, and we were involved with the political prisoners and the unemployed.

"When I finally got to college, I had already lived through many of the issues discussed there. I had sat through Christian-Marxist dialogs in our home. In sociolinguistics in college I learned about who says what, to whom, and when. But I had experienced that numerous times at our dining room table."

Surprised by Joy

I am surprised by joy—and grateful to God—for O-i's words. As I said already, much of the wisdom expressed here is hers, not mine. At times when I was working through the problems she mentioned, I was not aware that she was picking up such lasting principles from what Bob and I were doing. Ultimately all the good which she gained comes from the grace of God. Certainly I cannot take credit for the way my daughters have grown up. I had much help from friends, God's Spirit constantly gave Bob and me strength when we felt we were failing, and we both drew daily on the rich inheritance of values we had received from our parents.

Both our sets of parents drummed into us that we had to be honest about God. Grace is both the sign of God's love and forgiveness, and the gift of love which includes the ability to be honest. Since grace is poured out abundantly upon each of us, we encourage parents to share that grace generously with their children. Grace is the essential and visible mark of the Christian home.

5

SPIRITUAL DISCIPLINES: BUILDING STRENGTH IN THE HOME

As a little girl I learned about the spiritual discipline of prayer by watching my parents. My mother would kneel in the living room with her face buried in an easy chair. Meanwhile we children were allowed to romp around her. We could climb on her back, take off her shoes and even tickle her toes. But we could not talk to her because she was talking to Jesus. It seemed sometimes as though she was on her knees for hours, and a holy awe filled the room. We knew she was talking to Someone very important whom she loved very much.

And I remember my father walking up and down the length of our living room with his eyes half-open, praying. We could also play and talk around him, but not to him. He was talking to God. We couldn't explain it, but we could sense the divine Presence in the room.

My husband shares a similar background. It dawned on him as a little boy that when his grandmother knelt by her bed and poured out her heart in Swedish, she was talking to the Almighty God. Her door would be half open and he would stand there, listening. What a rich heritage our parents and grandparents have left us!

In *Celebration of Discipline* Richard Foster describes for modern readers how the classical spiritual disciplines can be practiced today to draw closer to God.[1] I would encourage each reader to delve into Foster's book. There you will find the help you need to put these spiritual exercises into practice in your own life. My purpose here is not to duplicate what Foster has already done so well. Instead, I want to focus on just a few of the classical disciplines and show how they can be used in family life and what difference they can make there.

We need to remember that our free salvation cost Jesus everything. But the paradoxical implication of free grace is that it will cost me everything I've got, "for whoever would save his life will lose it, and whoever loses his life for my sake will find it," said Jesus (Mt 16:25). That's why we must be willing to make big sacrifices in time and energy to draw closer to God. Only as we spend time in the presence of a holy God will we absorb the essence of a holy life. And without a life growing toward holiness we cannot become role models to our children.

Time with God
The irony of our day is that while society breaks down around us, our nation is preoccupied with conquering outer space. Since the explorers in centuries past have discovered all the territory on Earth, outer space seems like the next step. But perhaps the most neglected territory that needs to be invaded is our inner space.

The Bible makes it clear that individuals who want to be close to God must spend time with him on a regular basis. If we want to know God we must listen to him, read his Word, and talk to him. Meditation, Bible study and prayer are very important for modern

Christians trying to survive in our sick society. These disciplines are like lifelines keeping us tied into the security of God. But many of us are too busy to take the time for such things.

How left out our Savior must feel when so many of us are too busy to include our best Friend in the important things we have to do. We are so much like the Christians of Laodicea, "neither hot nor cold" in our love for Jesus. That's why Jesus had to say to them, "Behold, I stand at the door and knock; if any one hears my voice and opens the door, I will come in to him and eat with him, and he with me" (Rev 3:20). This is the call of Jesus' heart for intimacy with us.

Part of this being close to God means trying to keep him in the center of our thoughts even when we are not praying or reading his Word. Brother Lawrence, who lived in the seventeenth century, knew this type of intimacy with God. As a monk whose work was cooking, he wrote: "The time of business does not with me differ from the time of prayer; and in the noise and clatter of my kitchen, while several persons are at the same time calling for different things, I possess God in as great tranquillity as if I were upon my knees at the blessed sacrament."[2]

From my own experience I have found an amazing relationship between the quiet times of prayer and reading, and the practice of God's presence while doing other work. The more free of distraction my time alone with God is, the easier it is to continue to communicate with God throughout the work hours. And the more I experience God's presence in the noise and bustle of daily life, the more prepared I am to dispose myself at the end of the day.

This brings us to the first benefit that time with God gives to the family: It reminds us of God's presence. If I have spent time in prayer and Bible study, and if I am staying tuned to God all through the day, isn't that going to make a big difference in how I conduct my days? If I am thinking regularly about God, what effect might it have when I am tired and angry and tempted to berate my child for doing something wrong? And if I have spent a sleepless night comforting a sick child, and then I take time (while my spouse cares for the child) to commune with God, won't that help to heal my frazzled and sleepy nerves?

Time with God also gives us a chance to refill our spiritual and emotional reservoirs. We all need time for renewing our strength. The life of Jesus reflects a rhythm between prayer and activity:

That evening, at sundown, they brought to him all who were sick or possessed with demons. . . . And he healed many who were sick with various diseases, and cast out many demons; . . . And in the morning, a great while before day, he rose and went out to a lonely place, and there he prayed. And Simon and those who were with him pursued him, and they found him and said to him, "Everyone is searching for you." And he said to them, "Let us go to the next towns, that I may preach there also" (Mk 1:32-38).

Henri Nouwen has an interesting commentary on this passage:

In the middle of sentences loaded with action—healing suffering people, casting out devils, responding to impatient disciples, traveling from town to town and preaching . . . we find these quiet words: "In the morning, long before dawn, he got up and left the house, and went off to a lonely place and prayed there." In the center of breathless activities we hear a restful breathing. Surrounded by hours of moving we find a moment of quiet stillness. . . . The more I read this nearly silent sentence locked in between loud words of action, the more I have the sense that the secret of Jesus' ministry is hidden in that lonely place where he went to pray, early in the morning, long before dawn.[3]

If Jesus needed that time alone with God before the day started, we are audacious to think we can make it on our own without that. Just to survive as parents in today's world, we need a time of quiet.

Third, taking time for God also provides a good model for our children—a direct model of how to be close to our Savior. I began this chapter by talking about how I learned to pray by watching my parents do so regularly.

I can still remember when my elder brother Edvard, at age seven in our home in China, decided to have devotions. He got the idea from my father who was always up at 5 A.M. to pray and read his Bible. As a little sister, I in turn copied Edvard. It was contagious.

The same happened with the next generation. I find recorded in the back of my *Daily Light:* "May 12, I give thanksgiving— Before 7 A.M. both kids were in bed reading their Bibles. 'Surely goodness and mercy . . .' " How happy I was that May morning when I found my children communing with God.

Years later after Bob had built the house we now live in, I was calling upstairs for Kirsten to help with some chore. There was no answer, and I wondered where she was. Running upstairs to check, I found her out on the porch—beyond earshot—alone with her Bible. Again I was awed. I tiptoed back downstairs with a heart full of thanks to God that my daughter had found a secret place in our new home to meet God.

When I have a moment of inactivity, such as when I'm driving or waiting for an appointment, I frequently use these times for meditation, for example to imagine myself in the role of some biblical character—Mary or Martha, Peter or Thomas, Nicodemus or the woman of Samaria, Mary Magdalene or the Syro-Phoenecian woman, Matthew or Zacchaeus. Thus I experience Christ meeting me as he met these people long ago. I ask God to sanctify my imagination as I work through the drama of encountering Jesus in the shoes of the Gospel characters.

Often when the children were home, one of them would ask me at such times, "What are you thinking about, Mother?" Of course I was happy for the opportunity to share my thoughts and to describe for my children the ways in which I communicated with God. I cherished the opportunity to be a model for them.

The Transforming Union with Christ

But what about the times when my actions spoke louder than my words and I was not a good model to my children? There is a link here between the quality of my time with God and the quality of my daily life. When my devotional life is dry, patience with my children also tends to run short.

My goal is to deepen the communication I have with God. I do not want to simply read my Bible and recite a shopping list of prayers. Intellectual curiosity and intercession are not the main reasons for meeting with God. We are to meet with God the way two lovers meet with each other. When we are in love, we want to be in each other's presence. In the same way that we praise the object of our human love, we ought to praise God who surpasses any human being. Just thinking of the attributes of God releases us to praise—as we see so clearly in the Psalms.

And just as I listen to the human being I love and not just carry on a monologue, I need to listen to God, taking the time to let him speak to me in quietness. If I love God, I will enjoy just sitting in the presence of the Divine Lover in silence. I will be glad to lavish my love—and time—on my Savior.

After a concentrated time spent in God's presence, I find it easier to continue to walk with God throughout the day. This means communicating with God in whatever I'm doing—even when my tasks require my full concentration. God is there for us, and we can stop regularly for a second and recognize his presence. This will help us to lead a holy life, both with our children and away from them.

One of the regrets I have from my own years of parenting is that, while I had my daily time with God, this did not always carry over into a daily walk with God. Our lives were so busy with visitors, ministry opportunities, and correspondence with people around the world, that sometimes I was too busy for God *and* for my children. Then I would get tense when they misbehaved because they wanted attention. I lost my temper instead of recognizing that the problem was in me, not them.

The problem was not just a matter of having too much to do but of not abiding in God's presence as Jesus says we should in John 15. We are invited to interact with God moment by moment throughout each day.

Since my youngest child left home for college ten years ago, life has continued to be just as busy as before. In addition to being a pastor's wife, cooking for house guests, and babysitting grandchildren, I have started writing and speaking in many places, and have become involved with Muslim women. The busier I am, the more I need to withdraw daily as well as at retreat centers like the Praise of His Glory Ministries (277-14th Ave. NW, New Brighton, MN 55112). At these centers I have met young mothers and fathers who have taken a weekend off to listen to God. What better way to become the parents God wants us to be?

We must all balance a life of action in the world with a life of prayer in the inner sanctuary of the soul. The details of how this can be worked into busy schedules will be different for each person. But without this we will have trouble being good models for our children.

I like to encourage people to consider giving more than just half an hour or an hour to prayer each day. The more time we can spend in solitude with God, the more able we will be to face each day and to continue to commune with God. I avoid listening to the evening news—as I used to do—because I want to go to sleep with the goodness of God's love uppermost in my mind. And when I wake up, I want to first fix my mind and heart on the Good News before I get the bad news from my radio. Then when I hear the daily reports, I am more ready to intercede prayerfully for those who are hurting in the world.

This concentration on the Almighty is what Paul was talking about when he told us to pray without ceasing (1 Tim 5:17). It is also what the psalmist meant when he wrote "In thy presence is fulness of joy, at thy right hand are pleasures for evermore" (Ps 16:11). When we spend time in God's presence, we are changed—changed into better parents.

As Donald Coggan, the Archbishop of Canterbury, has said so well, "I go through life as a transient on his way to eternity, made in the image of God but with that image debased, needing to be taught how to meditate, to worship, to think."4 Through spending time with God I am directed to work on some aspect of my character, to change my attitude toward some circumstance, to grow more mature in my relationships to God and to others.

Much confusion in the areas of morals and ethics would be cleared up in Christian homes if family members knew how to meditate on God's Word (Ps 1:1-3; Josh 1:8). In our age of appliances, if something does not work, we frantically hunt for the manual to show us what has gone wrong. But we are living in a sick society with a handicapped, culture-bound church. We need to get back to God's Manual to see what has gone wrong.

One way to encourage Bible knowledge is to memorize Scripture as a family. This benefits both generations in the household. I am grateful for every verse I memorized when I was younger. It's much harder to memorize as a grandma! When the children were home, we all worked on the Navigators memory system—a good place to start—and also wrote our own verses on cards and kept them in a basket at the table for review during mealtime. The Word of God is now stored in our hearts for the Holy Spirit to use in our lives to keep us from sin (Ps 119:9-11).

Confession

We now turn from the more personal and inward disciplines to those that are done corporately in the body of Christ, the church. Since the family is a microcosm of the church, we will focus on how these disciplines are practiced within this "domestic church."

"Confess your sins to one another, and pray for one another, that you may be healed," James told the early church (5:16). In our individualistic society where one's relationship with God is supposed to be one's private affair, we have missed the wealth of blessing available in confessing to one another. Because there had been abuses in the medieval church, the reformers encouraged believers to confess to God alone. Of course God alone forgives sin, but we can be the instruments of bringing assurance of forgiveness to a troubled or doubting soul.

I am grateful for family members who have ministered to me in this way as I have confessed my sins, my doubts, and my hang- ups. I have confessed at times to my parents, brothers, sister-in-law, husband and children. For example, before we prayed together at night, I used to sit at the bedside of my children and give them time to review the day's events. Sins were often confessed. I confessed and they confessed. Those were very holy moments of the day when the slate was wiped clean between us and our God and between each other.

Writer Margaret Jensen describes her own childhood in similar ways. Before her mother tucked her in for the night, they would talk:

Every detail of school and play came up on the bedtime screen. Nothing was hidden from Mama. As she tucked me in, she always said, "Look at me, Margaret. Is there anything you need to tell me before we talk to God?" Knowing her secret line to God, the confessions poured out, and forgiveness followed. Sleep was sweet.[5]

For me this was not just a matter of a child confessing to a parent. Often I would have to ask forgiveness for wrongs I had done to my children. I remember one day in particular when I asked O-i to go for a walk with me after I had lost my temper. "Will you forgive Mama for having been angry with you when I shouldn't have been?" I asked.

"Of course I forgive you, Mama," seven-year-old O-i answered with her freckled face turned up to mine. Anger was often something with which I had to wrestle.

Such confession is more than therapeutic catharsis. We have not only confessed to each other, but we have confessed to the Christ who absorbed our anger, our hurt, our fear, our hostility in his wounds on the cross. Through confession we are healed and transformed within—with the help of family members who agonize and rejoice with us. Forgiveness brings rejoicing, for "if we walk in the light, as he is in the light, we have fellowship with one another, and the blood of Jesus his son cleanses us from all sin" (1 Jn 1:7).

Dietrich Bonhoeffer has a special insight into what walking in the light means:

A man who confesses his sins in the presence of a brother knows that he is no longer alone with himself; he experiences the presence of God in the reality of the other person. As long as I am by myself in the confession of my sins everything remains in the dark, but in the presence of a brother the sin has to be brought into the light.[6]

Perhaps we resent having others know about our sins because we think the church is for saints rather than sinners. We cover up our unresolved problems by heading for church with our Sunday-go-to-meeting smiles. And when we get home, we decide that confrontation is too painful, and so we bury our resentments of spouses, parents or children. No wonder John says, "We deceive ourselves and the truth is not in us" (1 Jn 1:8).

In America we pay a huge price for such deception—with broken homes and broken parent/child relationships. We need to ask ourselves, "Why did Jesus die?" Was it for beautiful homes and church buildings? Or was it to restore broken relationships?

Matthew 5:23-24 tells us to go quickly and make things right if there is a fractured relationship. We are not given the option of leaving such a problem in the darkness of our private world. We are to bring it out into the light. Pretense is our worst enemy. In our homes, our greatest need is not to get the house clean, but to bring out the dirt in our hearts and let Jesus scrub it clean with his blood.

Family Worship
One context in which confession and honesty can take place is in family worship. It is possible to take part in corporate worship at church and yet walk in darkness if our spirit has not been touched by God. But in family worship the stakes are higher and the closeness more intense. So it is more difficult to hide my honest feelings. In worshiping with my family I may be convicted to change some

outward action, or God's Spirit may touch my emotions so that I cry or laugh, or my mind may be stimulated to study further the Bible reading of the day.

Jesus draws us to himself when lifted up on the cross (Jn 12:32). We are not more or less drawn to Jesus when we are in a cathedral than when we are home, for Jesus has promised to be present whenever two or three believers meet to worship. Worship has nothing to do with the external setting, but it is our response to God's overtures of love. "[Worship] is kindled within us only when the Spirit of God touches our human spirit. Forms and rituals do not produce worship, nor does the formal disuse of forms and rituals. . . . Singing, praying, praising all may lead to worship, but worship is more than any of them. Our spirits must be ignited by divine fire."[7]

I can look back to times of family worship in my childhood home, as well as in the home Bob and I have established, when our spirits have been ignited with the divine fire. And we have commented like the disciples on the Emmaus road: "Did not our hearts burn within us while he talked to us?" (Lk 24:32)

While in the Philippines as a family, we did not always visit a local church on Sunday when on vacation (since we spent so much time in church the rest of the year). Instead we let our children plan an hour-long worship just for the family. With a flourish they produced everything from bulletins to offerings, special music and sermonettes. With plenty of humor interspersed in the proceedings, we nevertheless felt a holy awe during those worship times.

It was during one of those vacation family worship times that our eldest daughter had her first communion. Her father had prepared her by going through the Westminster Catechism, and the whole group of us celebrated this special privilege with her.

Since then I have often wondered why the modern church does not encourage partaking of the Lord's Supper in the home. In the book of Acts the two times when the communion service is mentioned, it is in the home (2:46 and 20:7). Since the church started in the homes of believers, there was not the distinction we have today of formal worship in the church and family worship in the home. But perhaps we need to get back to the reality that the home is where Christian formation takes place among our children. Hence, it can be a good place to celebrate the Lord's Table. (In order to avoid possible problems, perhaps such home communions could be done under the auspices of the local church to which the family belongs.)

Communion in the home can also bring healing to the family, for the clearest expression of Christian community is to be found in Holy Communion. . . . Being members of one body, we eat of one bread and drink of one cup, the solemn guarantee of our eternal relationship with God and with one another. . . . It is here that we sort out our relationships with one another. If we fail to do that, we shall be "guilty of profaning the body and blood of the Lord."[8]

Thomas à Kempis also wrote about the importance of communion in *The Imitation of Christ,* for five hundred years the most widely read devotional book in the world. He warns us across the ages, "The Enemy, knowing the exceeding great profit and healing which lies in the holy communion, endeavors by every means and occasion to the utmost of his power to withdraw and hinder faithful and devout persons from partaking." He goes on to talk of the believer's being inflamed with the love of Christ at the table of the Lord.[9]

With these words in mind, we as parents have to look on ourselves as the royal priesthood in the home (1 Pet 2:9). We are the ones who are finally responsible for our children's spiritual welfare. When we give an account to God on how we trained them in the faith, we cannot stand before the Almighty and blame the pastor or youth worker for the lack of spiritual input in our child's life.

Guidance
Seeking the guidance of God is another spiritual discipline which needs to be practiced more openly in the home. Children benefit

when we involve them in the decision-making process. This does not mean that we form a committee and vote on what we should do. Listening to the voice of God is radically different from the democratic process. I believe that if we as a family sincerely ask God to show us the way we should go, God will honor our prayer and answer us.

We prayed with our children about many decisions, including what schools they should go to, when we should ask for furlough, and whether we should leave the Philippines to join my mother when she was ill in Norway. Often for us adults, fasting and prayer went together, as in Acts: "While they were worshiping the Lord and fasting, the Holy Spirit said . . ."(13:2-3). The answer always came—as God had promised.

But not all prayers for guidance should be shared with the children. For instance, Bob's parents started praying the day he was born that he would become a missionary. But they never told him about this prayer. Only when he told them about his call from God did they share how they had been praying all those years. How over-joyed they were when they sent us off to the Philippines!

Celebration

When the will of God is known for the big decisions in life, this is cause for celebration. In the home in which I grew up, every Sunday was a celebration. We dressed for a party as soon as we jumped out of bed, and we came to breakfast for a special menu where even the grace was different. Instead of the usual boiled eggs and "I Jesus navn gaar vi til bords" [in Jesus' name we come to the table] we sang in English, "Safely through another week, God has led us on our way," and ate imported cornflakes which had traveled for weeks on the back of mules to reach us in far-off Shanxi, China.

In the nest that Bob and I have built, the same song has been sung for over thirty years, and the same efforts made to preserve Sunday as a day of celebration.

From Sunday dinners and coffee parties with sugar lumps, to

Easter, Thanksgiving and Christmas, we have opportunities for Christian families to stop to rest and celebrate on the journey of faith. In Old Testament times the Israelites had feasts: they remembered the exodus at the Feast of the Passover in the spring, they renewed their covenant with God at the Feast of Pentecost in early summer, and they thanked God for being a blessed people at the Feast of Tabernacles in the fall.

These were times of celebration when they took the long journey to Jerusalem, the highest city geographically. This became their metaphorical journey to the City of God. As they walked they sang the Songs of Ascents (Psalms 120-134). They were like walking songs to remind them who they were and where they were going. "This picture of the Hebrews singing [and making] . . . their way from towns and villages . . . up to Jerusalem has become embedded in the Christian devotional imagination. It is our best background for understanding life as a faith-journey," writes Eugene Peterson.[10]

We all remember when Jesus as a boy joined his parents for one of these journeys to Jerusalem. Later, when he announced his earthly ministry, he called it a celebration—the Year of Jubilee—when captives would be released, the blind see and the poor hear good news (Lk 4:18-19). All through his earthly ministry, Jesus had days of joyful celebration with his disciples, eating and drinking in the homes of his friends. But the great difference between Jesus and us lies in his constant obedience to the Father (Jn 6:38). If we want to follow in his steps, we have to learn what the old hymn says, "Trust and obey, for there's no other way to be happy in Jesus, but to trust and obey."

There are many ways to express that joy. Psalm 150 suggests celebrating God's goodness with trumpet, lute, harp, timbrel and dance, with strings, pipe and loud clashing cymbals. At the exodus we find Miriam leading God's people in a great celebration dance (Ex 15:20), and later we find David leaping and dancing before the Lord (2 Sam 6:14, 16).

Bob and I have had the joy of learning Norwegian folk dancing

in the last few years. We have found this a wonderful way of express-
ing our inner joy in God's goodness to us as a couple. We also enjoy
singing together. Our family reunions are usually marked by singing, especially when either of my brothers, Hakon or Torje, are
present to play the piano. We can sing for hours, going through the
old hymnbooks from childhood. Such celebration has always
played an important part in our journey of faith as a family.

A family that can celebrate together, praising God for his goodness and thanking him for each other, will be better able to with-
stand trial and suffering when they come. This foundation of praise
is needed to keep us from developing a bitter spirit when we face
great difficulties.

Just recently we had an evening of celebration which was a great
gift of healing after having gone through some heartaches both at
church and in our extended family. Our granddaughter Sara turned
two, and the whole family gathered at her Aunt O-i's and Uncle
Ross's house for the party. Since Sara loves our piano but doesn't
have one at her house, Bob and I gave her a toy baby grand. She
was immediately mesmerized by the sound it made, giggling to
herself and clapping her hands. She seemed to know that music was
for celebration.

Meanwhile, big sister Elisa was feeling a bit left out, so Grandpa
put her on his lap to tell her a story of "Once upon a time long,
long ago . . ." At age seven he had visited his grandmother's farm
in the north, and his great-uncle, who was bringing a team of horses
in for the night, offered little Bobby the driver's seat and the reins.
It was the greatest moment of his life as he proudly drove that team
of six huge horses into the barn.

I watched the adults' attention shifting back and forth between
the happy little girl snuggled in Grandpa's lap—while he relived his
childhood—and the birthday celebrant making a "joyful noise unto
the Lord" on the floor. Truly, the little child was leading them, even
in celebration.

6

NURTURING YOUNG DISCIPLES

In ERMA BOMBECK'S SUBURBIA THE women are so lonely that they talk to their tropical fish. "You become about as exciting as your food blender. The kids come in, look you in the eye, and ask if anybody's home," says Erma.[1] The children are so secure in the knowledge that mother is always home that they can afford to ignore her as a person.

In another suburban community center I watch an attractive young mother who is lost in the rhythm of an aerobics class. Her well-formed body glides gracefully to the quick beat, while at her feet her two-year-old is trying to mimic her movements.

"Go back and sit on the floor!" the pretty mother scolds. The little girl huddles against the wall, scared and hurt. It's apparently not the first time this child has known rejection.

Next, we go back to the Philippines where my friend Inday is asking me about family planning. After attending my classes and going to the doctor's appointment, she confides, "I just don't know. You see, when I have my baby that's the only time something out of the ordinary is happening. I look forward to it all year." She goes on to have thirteen children. Food is scarce, but there's plenty of love and acceptance for each one.

And on to Norway, where my seventy-year-old friend tells me how she had to leave home at fourteen to go to work as a domestic in a nearby town. One day she was crying over a letter from home. Her employer, a well-respected and kindly gentleman, ran upstairs and asked sympathetically, "I'm so sorry. Has somebody died at home?" "No, another one was born! Now we are ten," she sobbed.

The children from these four homes have one thing in common. They were all involved in life's big questions—even before they were born. While one child is so sure of his identity at home that he can treat his mother like a fixture around the house, the other feels very unsure of herself with her mother. And while one set of children feel safe in their mother's love—even in the midst of unimaginable poverty—another child of poverty feels overwhelmed by the responsibility of another mouth to feed.

These true stories, like the stories of children all around the world—regardless of race or riches—raise the same questions:

Who am I?

Where did I come from?

Where am I going?

Why am I here?

Who cares?

In *Women at the Crossroads,* I tell the story of my own identity crisis as a teen-ager in a prison camp during World War 2 in China.[2] I had many questions: Who am I? A number that I repeat twice a day during roll call? If I'm important to God, why am I in this prison? Why is there so much suffering in the world?

I am grateful that I was forced by circumstances I would never have chosen to answer these questions early in life. And kids today all around the world are also being forced to answer the same questions. Circumstances may vary, but usually they are not of our choosing. Even in the affluent West, childhood is no idyllic holiday excursion to adulthood.

Who Am I?

Am I a latchkey kid? A child of divorce? A girl with buck teeth? A guy with big ears? An illegitimate child? A welfare kid?

While all these identification marks loom large in a child's mind, none of them determines the identity of a human being created in the image of God. This is where parents make all the difference. Christian parents have the unique privilege of imparting to their children in a hundred different ways the knowledge that they are greatly loved by the God who created them and chose this special family for them to belong to during their pilgrimage on earth. God's acceptance of a child is most powerfully communicated through the parents' love and acceptance. And, when children grow up in the loving atmosphere of a Christian home, they will also spontaneously learn to love and accept themselves without any planned self-esteem course to aid the process.

Right now, I'm watching this drama unfold in my four-year-old grandchild. She lights up at the words, "I love you," or "Jesus loves you." It's fun to hear her respond, "I love you too." Or watch her cuddle up to her baby sister, "I love you, Sara."

Long before she is old enough to be taught the two great Christian commandments, she is beginning to experience what it means to love God through Jesus and to love the people who inhabit her little world. She can love others as she loves herself because she has been accepted by those around her. With beautiful abandonment she flings her arms around her bearded grandpa and tells him she loves him. She is finding herself as she loses herself in those she loves.

By contrast, the child who experiences rejection turns inward, away from people, for fear of being hurt again. Thus rejection leads to low self-esteem and eventually to the "I hate myself" syndrome.

If I hate myself, created in the image of God, the next step is to hate another human being, also created in God's image.

Robert Vernon, a Los Angeles cop, has watched this drama unfold over and over again: "Detesting one's self makes it impossible to honor, respect, or love others. From such a perspective it is then easy to extinguish or destroy something that has little value. . . . This hostility is another explanation for the brutal, often pointless, acts of violence. . . . Having dealt with individuals displaying these symptoms over my 26 years as a police officer, there is no question in my mind that the self-image is formed early in life. Further, behavior that stems from low self-esteem often understandably results in more rejection. . . . It follows, then, that the key to analyzing this complex problem lies in the home—that institution primarily responsible for socializing new human beings."[3]

The LA cop goes on to tell us how often he calls to inform parents that their juvenile is in trouble and finds no one home. He singles out absentee parents as a major cause of the problems he sees. How can a relationship of love be built when parents are constantly turning their children over to others to be raised? In this day of dual-income parents, we need to think about the effect this may have on our children. One concern is the simple feeling of rejection that children may feel when their parents leave them with someone else each day.

Most parents do not realize how early their children begin to miss them. Pediatricians call these symptoms "separation anxiety." My sister-in-law, Dr. Karen Olness, suggests:

If both parents plan to work outside the home and leave their baby with someone who is not a usual member of the household, this preferably should be arranged before six to seven months of age or after two years. A child who has never been left with a stranger and is suddenly separated from parents at the age of eighteen months may be severely traumatized. . . . Separation anxiety wanes after twenty-four months, and normal children usually separate easily from their mothers at least for brief periods by three years.[4]

Other pediatricians suggest that separation anxiety can be acute for the three or four-year-old as well. But all agree that a child starts to feel accepted or rejected at an early age, and when rejection is followed by more rejection over a period of years, children will be emotionally scarred.

Therapist Scott Peck tells of such a person.[5] This brilliant but unsuccessful computer technician sought counseling when he was in his early thirties. His wife had left him, taking their two children. She complained that he was jealous of her, cold and unstable.

This man had dropped out of college. He had never been able to advance in his field or even keep a job because he could not get along with his supervisors. His most frequent expression was, "You can't trust a _____ soul."

He said his childhood had been normal and his parents fairly average, yet he remembered many instances from his youth when his parents let him down. They promised him a bicycle for his birthday, for instance, but forgot about it. Once they forgot his birthday entirely. They often promised to do things with him on weekends but then said they were too busy. They would even forget to pick him up from meetings or parties because "they had a lot on their minds."

Gradually this man came to the conclusion that he simply could not trust his parents. Once he came to that realization, his disappointments diminished. But this assumption set the stage for his later problems. To a child, parents represent the universe. So the conclusion this fellow actually came to was not, "I can't trust my parents," but "I can't trust people." Thus all authority figures could not be trusted, and this included teachers, police and employers.

Unfortunately, children are often wounded for life because few of us are aware—when we start parenting—what a tremendous responsibility is ours to provide an atmosphere of love, acceptance and trust for each child. We fail to count the cost in hours and emotional energy and resources. It's too easy to treat our children like live dolls—someone we can play with when we're in the right mood, and leave for someone else to play with when we're busy.

My husband and I greatly admire two couples we know who have decided not to have children. With their sense of calling to serve others in their professions, both couples know they could not provide the necessary atmosphere of love and acceptance that children need. How much better to count the cost before they start, rather than plunge in and later discover that their children are marred for life because the parents were not around when they were needed.

On the other hand, when children are nurtured in a home where they know they are loved and accepted by God and their parents, they become secure in their identity as people who are greatly loved. This truth enables them to respond by loving and trusting God, themselves, their parents, and others.

With the breakdown of the family, such truth is forced upon us with renewed urgency. It has led the producer of the Synopsis of Youth Film Series to say, "For too long, young people have been told that their greatest problems are drugs, sex, alcohol, etc. . . . These are, in fact, only symptoms of a much greater disease. The disease of youth is [that key relationships] are in disarray—their relationships with God, self, parents, friends, and the world."[6] For children, as for adults, it is only in relationships that we know our true identity and can answer the searching question: "Who am I?"

Where Did I Come From?

The second question is closely tied to the first and has already been partially answered. A child in a Christian home will be taught early in life that a good God created "all things bright and beautiful, all creatures great and small." Snuggled in the arms of one of the parents, the child will be told, "You see, we asked God to give us a very special baby all our own, and one happy day he sent you to us."

If the children are adopted they can be told that they were chosen and waited for with great expectation longer than any natural children. The details of biological birth are not as important as the divine origin—we came from the creative hands of God. Opening the Bible we can share some of God's own explanations: "Before I formed you in the womb I knew you, and before you were born I consecrated you" (Jer 1:5). Or David's outburst of gratitude for knowing where he came from:

Thy eyes beheld my unformed substance;
   in thy book were written, every one of them,
the days that were formed for me,
   when as yet there was none of them.
How precious to me are thy thoughts . . .
   How vast is the sum of them! (Ps 139:16-17)

David was very sure of himself. He knew who he was and where he came from. This prepared him for the great task of ruling God's chosen people. When Samuel was sent to the home of Jesse to look for a king, the prophet thought Eliab was God's choice. But he was wrong: "Do not look on his appearance or on the height of his stature, because I have rejected him; for the LORD sees not as man sees; man looks on the outward appearance, but the LORD looks on the heart" (1 Sam 16:7).

We all tend to look at the outside. How many teen-agers have not hated themselves one minute and loved themselves the next, as they look in the mirror. It's so human to compare ourselves to sports heroes, TV personalities and pop singers, and envy not only their performance, but their good looks.

But what a boring world if we all looked alike! The wonder of creation lies in the fact that not a snowflake, fingerprint, or human face is like any other. Each of us has been custom-made. Each is an original creation. We need to share with our children early in life that God made them just right—each a unique design—with just the right nose, hair, eyes, height, body-build and intelligence.

"Since God made only one of you, you are needed to reflect your Creator just the way you are," we must repeat to our children often. For to say otherwise is to insult my Maker, the Creator of this work of art which is me. We need to positively reinforce our children to help them memorize at an early age and then review often what God has to say about them from the Bible:

> But now thus says the LORD,
>> he who created you, . . .
> "Fear not, for I have redeemed you;
>> I have called you by name, you are mine. . . .
> Because you are precious in my eyes,
>> and honored, and I love you." (Is 43:1, 4)

This is all part of establishing our divine origin. Of course the time will also come when children will ask about their biological origins. Besides giving them as much of "the facts of life" as they are ready for, we can use this opportunity to bathe their conception—the first time they were thought of—in love. It was because father and mother loved each other so much that the consummation took place and the child was conceived.

I remember telling each of my children how we celebrated their conceptions with a party as soon as I found out I was pregnant. Their eyes lit up to think they were that important when they were just a tiny, tiny speck in my womb. In those moments of awe and wonder it is easy to turn a child's attention to the God who puts love into our hearts for each other. My first-born's favorite childhood book asks the big question: "Who put the love in Mommy's eyes and Daddy's too?"

"God does."[7]

Now that same book is a favorite of her first child, and so the good news is passed on from generation to generation.

Where Am I Going?

As believers we know that, just as we have come from God, so we will also return to God. I embraced this truth so early in life that it's hard for me to understand how so many young people from Christian homes can miss it. The first book I read in the English language was John Bunyan's *Pilgrim's Progress,* which made a profound impression on me. We knew where we were going, as the familiar song goes,

This world is not my home;
I'm just a passing through.
If heaven's not my home,
Then Lord what will I do?
The angels beckon me from heaven's open door,
And I can't feel at home in this world anymore.[8]

The complex subject of death cannot be relegated to a unit in the Sunday-school curriculum. If children are around adults who long to see Jesus face to face, their outlook on life and death will be turned upside down. As parents, we model a Christian attitude toward death which is caught, not taught. Are we terrified of death? Or do we look on it as an escape from life? There is no way we can disguise inappropriate feelings from our children. Only as we can answer the question, "Where am I going?" for ourselves can we be of any help to them.

Paradoxically, our children have an advantage over us. They are more open to truth about the God's kingdom than we are. Their imaginations have not been tainted with doubts about the reality of heaven. That's why Jesus told us, "Unless you turn and become like children, you will never enter the kingdom of heaven" (Mt 18:3).

If as adults we know where we are going, we can look on Christian funerals as an opportunity to demonstrate to our children that while we will miss the loved ones that go ahead of us on the pilgrimage, and while death is not what God originally intended for his people, we can be joyful for those who have found happiness in another life with their Lord and Savior. We sang often as missionary children in China:

Around the throne of God in heaven
Thousands of children stand
Children whose sins are all forgiven
A holy, happy band:

Singing glory, glory, glory.

On earth they sought the Savior's grace,
On earth they loved His Name;
So now they see his blessed face,
And stand before the Lamb:
Singing glory, glory, glory.[9]

Some theologians have suggested that when Jesus says about children—"for to such belongs the kingdom of heaven" (Mt 19:14)—he is referring to all the children who have died before they reach the age of accountability and have gone ahead of us to the City of God. Is he telling us indirectly that there will be more children than adults in heaven?

Bishop William Cox of the Episcopal Church preached a sermon recently on all the children who inhabit heaven. My friend Bob McKewin writes, "He spoke of our need to recognize that all human life is precious to Almighty God. Our children who die young, miscarriages, abortions, full term children who die in the first moments after birth . . . are all reared in heaven by Jesus and the angels. Bishop Cox is a loving and caring man. As he spoke, it was obvious to us that the God he serves, our God, is even more loving and caring."[10] That's what our children need to know.

Why Am I Here?

Just as we need to tell our children about the goodness that heaven holds for them, so we need to communicate to them their mission in life. We need to impart a sense of destiny to each child. Jesus said, "For this I was born, and for this I have come into the world, to bear witness to the truth" (Jn 18:37).

Each of us has to answer in our own way and in our own words why we are here. If God has made us all uniquely different, then there must be something specific for each of us to do. Children can be taught early about the gifts mentioned in Paul's and Peter's letters, and start thinking and praying about what gifts God may give them.[11]

Aptitude tests are one way of finding out what inborn abilities God has given us. The parable of the talents throws further light on our abilities—God has given some more talents than others. With this comes special responsibility, for Jesus says, "Every one to whom much is given, of him will much be required; and of him to whom men commit much they will demand the more" (Lk 12:48).

The point of the parable of the talents is that whether we have many assets or few, they are to be used for the service of God and our world. To bury a talent in the ground is the worst sin. The man in the story says, "I was afraid, and I went and hid your talent." Fear is the opposite of faith. Our children have abundant faith when they are very young. After a few hard knocks, they may begin to show signs of fear. They want to avoid being hurt again. This would be a good time to talk about the parable of the talents and what particular talent that child has to use in life.

When a child is encouraged to believe that God endowed him or her with special abilities for a special task that no one else can do, then because of faith in a good God, that child may study hard and develop those God-given abilities in order to use them in service to others. And more talents will be given to the faithful child, for Jesus promised, "To every one who has will more be given, and he will have abundance; but from him who has not, even what he has will be taken away" (Mt 25:29).

This message is especially important to communicate to girls who are often stereotyped at an early age. Girls need to hear from parents and other role models that God has a special mission for them to fulfill in life. While girls often take their studies more seriously than boys, when they reach a certain age they receive the unspoken message that their sex appeal is their greatest asset. They need to receive a clear vision of their priorities in life so that they will not be swayed by such talk.

I shall never forget the time O-i asked me at age eighteen: "Why are most of my models of Christian commitment men and not women?" I was delighted to have the opportunity to show her that many of the men she was admiring had dedicated their lives to some goals beyond themselves—to help others become all they were meant to be. It gave me the opportunity to remind her that her first priority was to give her whole self to Christ, who says:

> If anyone wishes to be a follower of mine, he or she must leave self behind. . . . and come with me. Whoever cares for his or her safety is lost; but if a boy or girl will be lost for my sake, he or she will find a true self. What will a boy or girl gain by winning the whole world, at the cost of his or her true self? (Mt 16:24-26, paraphrased)

Write this verse out on a card for your child, using the right gender to make it more personal for your boy or girl.

Who Cares?

Perhaps one of the most telling questions that children these days ask is, Who cares about me? We need to communicate to our children, mostly nonverbally, that our God never forsakes us nor hides from us. He is not the God of twentieth-century literature that has to be searched for and waited for.

If God seems hidden or distant, it's us who have moved. Because our God cared so much for Adam and Eve when they were hiding, the first big search for lost humanity started in the Garden of Eden. "Where are you?" is the first question asked in human history. The questioner is God, always on a search of love. Another song we used to sing as children was about the sheep that was lost (Mt 18:12-14):

> But none of the ransomed ever knew
> How deep were the waters crossed,
> Nor how dark was the night that the Lord passed through
> Ere He found His sheep that was lost.
> Out in the desert He heard its cry,
> Sick and helpless and ready to die.

But all through the mountains, thunder-riven,
And up from the rocky steep,
There arose a cry to the gate of heaven,
"Rejoice! I have found my sheep!"
And the angels echoed around the throne:
"Rejoice for the Lord brings back His own."[12]

This means that regardless of how far away from God I feel, nor how many others there are for God to look after, the gentle Shepherd is searching for me.

This theme of grace is the central message of the gospel, yet how often, even if it might be repeated over and over again in church, do we not hear it? For there is the accompanying message of works that so often drowns out the message of grace. Standing outside church during worship one morning, a man confided to my husband, "I don't think I'll bother to go in today. I'll just guard the parking lot. I know already what they're going to say: Be good, be good, be good!"

Our children also may hear this other message loud and clear. Why do they leave church when they feel far from God? Have they been absorbing a gospel of works instead of one of grace? It's easy for young people to leave church if they feel they cannot measure up to the impossible standards set by other Christians.

One Sunday at Hope Church we were greatly refreshed by John Staggers, sitting at the piano, and proclaiming in a beautiful, booming voice,

Jesus loves me when I'm good
When I do the things I should
Jesus loves me when I'm bad
Though it makes his great heart sad.

I wished then that all the people who had left church because they did not feel good enough could have been there.

Blessed are the children who come from Christian homes where they can hear the message of grace, not just one or two hours a week in church on Sunday, but 168 hours a week at home. In these families the children know that this world is not divided into good guys and bad guys. Life is not a melodrama where the hero always wins because he is good and the villain is caught because he is bad.

We are all sinners, and we are all responsible for the sin in the world. When the temptation comes to draw a circle that excludes the undesirable person, we need to draw a bigger circle of love to include the neighborhood nuisance or the outcast at church. Parents need to be models. We cannot throw a teaching at our children and expect them to work it out without having watched us handle the delicate dramas of life.

While we are helping another kid on the block, we are giving our own the greatest object lesson of their lives. They begin to see that God's love is unconditional, that the other child did not have to conform to Christian ideals before he was loved, and that none of us have to conform to be loved by either God or our parents. God is the most important Person who cares about us, and next in line comes our parents.

Discipline is perhaps the most important area for communicating a sense of security and unconditional love. I have a close friend who tells me her greatest sense of insecurity as a child came from the fact that there were no rules in her home. Her friends had to be home on time, but she didn't. This made her feel that her parents didn't care about her.

Another parent who was abused in childhood shares her experience as she has tried to distinguish between boundaries and abuse:

You must have a balanced approach to discipline in your home . . . certain things that are just not allowed. . . . That kind of discipline gives the kids a feeling of security. They know what the boundaries are. At the same time they know that you love them. That is why discipline should never be ignored, especially by parents who were abused as children. . . . Unfortunately, many of these parents go to the opposite extreme and never discipline their children because they were so badly beaten themselves. The results are children who know no boundaries.[13]

Boundaries are needed for the children's protection and as another way of saying, "I love you." This includes delicate areas like TV watching. I remember telling a group of women years ago that if my sixteen-year-old daughter is watching something harmful to her, it is my responsibility to turn the set off. Some were rather horrified and expressed fear that my daughter might rebel both against me and God. Thanks to our good Lord, she is still a devout Christian. And she and her new husband have just decided that they don't need a TV set in their home!

But boundaries were set long before she was sixteen. I remember having a babysitter who had a hard time getting shoes on our kids on a cold, wet day. They wanted to go barefoot and splash in the chilly mud. She told them in my hearing, "You better put your shoes on or your mother will be angry." I tried to tell her that that was a poor reason for getting a child to obey. It's not that I never got angry, but if I did I usually apologized and let them know that the way I expressed my anger was wrong. Any boundaries we set were an opportunity, not to tell our children we would be angry with them, but to tell them that we love them and don't want them to get hurt or sick.

Discipline was always—at least always intended to be—carried out in this spirit of love. If a child needed to be punished for some infraction, we tried to keep the punishments in line with the seriousness of the disobedience. And we certainly tried to make it clear that our love did not end when the bad behavior began. Our kids knew we still loved them even when we were very upset.

After disciplining our children we felt it was important to do something together, or at least to remain in the same room. We needed the chance to be close so that reconciliation could take place. When the girls were young they were glad to sit on our laps for a long time to feel close and secure again. When they got older it was more natural to suggest some activity that would draw us together—anything from a dish of ice cream to a swim at the beach twenty minutes away. Reconciliation needed to be followed by celebration.

This is all part of God's great unconditional love and grace poured out on us. It's only because of God's overwhelming grace that we and our children can find the answers to life's biggest problems: Who am I? Where did I come from? Where am I going? Why am I here? Who cares?

A beautiful story is told in Finland of a boy who stole candy in a store where his mother was shopping. His mother told him he would have to go to the storekeeper and confess and bring back the candy. The poor boy was in agony for days because he could not face such an ordeal. Then the father entered the conflict with another solution. He said he would go on the boy's behalf to the storekeeper and apologize for him and bring back the candy. The boy was overwhelmed and overjoyed at such a solution.

Of course, parents ought not to take responsibility for all of their children's bad behavior. If our kids don't face the consequences of their actions they may never properly mature. But when it is clear that a child has repented, then parents can follow the example of Jesus. He does not scold us for not measuring up to the standards of perfection set for us. Jesus steps in and takes the consequences. This is unmerited grace and the greatest truth we can pass on to our children.[14]

"It's grace that brought me safe thus far, and grace will lead me home"—all the way to the City of God.

7

THE BIG
ISSUES OF
GROWING UP

WE RETURNED FROM FURLOUGH one year just in time to enroll our children in the Philippine Women's College of Davao City. There one could start in kindergarten and graduate from college, all on the same campus. For our youngest it was the beginning of her school career. Every morning she lined up with the rest of the school to salute the Filipino flag and pray the Lord's Prayer and the "Hail Mary." When I had enrolled my children the principal had assured me that the Muslim and Protestant minorities were not expected to participate in Catholic rituals or religion classes.

But by the third day of school elder sister was worried! "O-i is already a Catholic," she reported. " I watched her this morning and she mumbled the 'Hail Mary' and even crossed herself." Kirsten had been standing tightlipped at attention like a good Protestant during the flag ceremony and checking to see what her little sister was doing.

I waited till evening when I usually had a bedside talk and prayer with the girls before kissing them good night.

"You know, I'm saying the 'Hail Mary'," came the confession. "I do it because all my classmates are doing it . . . and I know Jesus understands."

My husband and I had a good laugh about it that night and decided not to make an issue of it. In a few weeks O-i let us know that she had quit saying the "Hail Mary." She felt secure enough in her new environment not to.

"But she will form a habit of conforming to her environment rather than standing up for her convictions," argued a missionary friend. Another missionary was more concerned about my children pledging allegiance to a foreign country.

"It's just not right for an American to pledge allegiance to the Filipino flag," she argued.

"But we are guests in this country," I replied. "My children are not pledging their allegiance because they are Filipinos, but because they are showing respect for their host country. We are allowed to live here. This soil is our home for now."

Majoring on the Minor

These are two issues involving religious ritual and patriotism: Do these touch on major Christian values in the lives of our children? Or are other things more important? It's easy for all of us to major on the minor.

About ten years later, back in the States, a woman came for counseling at a retreat I was conducting: "I just don't know what to do about my sixteen-year-old. She refuses to conform to any standards of neatness. Every morning the bathroom looks like a cyclone hit it."

"What values do you want your child to take with her when she leaves home—maybe in two years?" I asked. Was it neatness? The mother shook her head.

"Why don't you just focus on a good relationship with your daughter?" I suggested. "Forget about the bathroom. It's too late for that. You want her heart and her confidence so she'll come to you when the big issues of life are in question."

One of the easiest things for parents to do—especially during the teen years—is to lose their perspective about their children. When they do that, they end up majoring on the minor issues in their child's life and perhaps losing their influence over the really important issues in life.

So what do I mean by the big issues or important values? Jesus' chief teachings deal with the values of the kingdom. Some of these values have already been touched on in the third chapter: God's view of power, money and sex. But here I want to look more closely at the priorities of God's kingdom and how those priorities can be worked out in our families.

The great thing about the values Jesus gives us in the Gospels is that he does not give them in theological propositions, but in images. So it's easy to pass them on to our children by using these stories and parables to make our point. Few children fail to enjoy good stories. Each story Jesus tells introduces a new principle.

These stories are good not just because they are fun to hear but also because they avoid a parent's natural tendency to give a child a list of do's and don'ts. We can all err by making lists and binding them around the necks of our children—with formulas promising heaven if they do the right thing at the right time, and hell if they don't. But that kind of legalism denies the first priority of God's kingdom, which is the grace that comes when we love and trust in God.

Kingdom Values for the Home

This first and most important aspect of God's value system is that the faith and love with which we respond to God comes from God in the first place. It is freely given.

Nothing is more important to impart to our children than the fact that we come to God every day of our lives bankrupt—with empty hands—to receive the free gift of grace. First we are given the faith we need to receive God's gift, then we receive God's grace, and after that God's love.

And once God's love is poured into our hearts (Rom 5:5), we love him back. We love because he first loved us. We receive from God even the love we have for him.

Because of God's tremendous love for us and the work of his grace, we need not fear him. Yet many children—and even adults—do. My husband remembers vividly the fear that would overwhelm him when his parents did not return home when they had said they would. He thought the rapture or Second Coming of Christ had taken place and he had been left behind—maybe he had not been good enough, or maybe he had not had the right kind of conversion experience to enter the kingdom.

Alvera Mickelsen of Bethel College has found that an astounding number of students from good Christian homes have lived with this fear. Others believe that their parents' divorce or some similar trauma took place because God is punishing them.

It is a sad commentary on the church and the family that the message of grace is not reaching our children. Home should be the first place where the child is introduced to God's upside-down value system. Children should know that we bring nothing to God but yet receive faith and love and forgiveness from him.

The second kingdom value is closely related to the first. Any child who knows the love, acceptance and forgiveness of God has a head start on loving and forgiving others. But it also works the other way around. Children who have not felt loved and accepted by their parents have a hard time feeling loved and accepted by God, and therefore also have trouble showing love and acceptance to others. It's really a cycle of love which can either start with knowing I am loved by God, or start with knowing I am loved by my parents.

There is no way we can love people outside the home, yet fail to show love and concern and forgiveness for those we are related to. Yet from the very first, men and women have struggled with relationships at home (Gen 4:9).

If love were just a feeling it would be easy. The alcoholic father believes he loves his family—on his own terms. While he has taken no responsibility for either babies or bills, he will sit in a bar and weep over how much he loves and misses his family. Love for him is a warm feeling and hot tears that demand no action.

When Jesus talked of love he talked of dying for another person (Jn 15:13). So how do we learn the value of giving our lives for another? Only by being around Jesus: "For the love of Christ controls us, because we are convinced that one has died for all; therefore all have died. And he died for all, that those who live might live no longer for themselves but for him who for their sake died and was raised" (2 Cor 5:14-15). Paul is saying that being around Jesus gives us a new set of values about giving our lives for someone else.

But this kind of sacrificial love is not the only love that keeps a family together. Families also need the everyday, common love of friendship. This means doing things with children, building memories of good times spent together. Perhaps we can change the slogan, "The family that prays together, stays together," to "The family that prays together and plays together, stays together."

The kingdom value of loving our family is closely related to the third value of loving our enemies. Often our greatest enemy is found within the walls of our home. Most of us do not develop strong dislikes for people we seldom see or with whom we do not have to interact on an intimate level. So our love is most tested in the home.

Could Jesus have been thinking of a modern home when he said, "If you love those who love you. . . . And if you do good to those who do good to you, what credit is that to you? For even sinners do the same. And if you lend to those from whom you hope to receive, what credit is that to you? . . . But love your enemies, and do good, and lend, expecting nothing in return; and your reward will be great, and you will be sons of the Most High; for he is kind to the ungrateful and the selfish. Be merciful, even as your Father is merciful" (Lk 6:32-36).

What do families quarrel over? Borrowing and lending, lack of forgiveness, condemning one another, refusing to do favors for fear of being used. Parents may feel that neither spouse nor children appreciate how hard they work. On the other hand, teen-agers may feel their requests for money or favors go unheeded. And so each blames the other that the harmony they once knew is no longer there.

What is missing is grace—the unmerited favor Jesus talks about. This value is so foreign to our way of thinking that we will need to review the lesson and find new areas of application in each stage of our children's growth. But if we learn to love the difficult child, spouse or sibling at home, it will be a cinch to learn to love those we do not have to live with day in and day out. And we will be better able to teach our children how to love others.

There will be times when we will have to help our children to love that "unfair" teacher, that obnoxious classmate or that impossible kid next door. These are the golden opportunities to pray and discuss the words of Jesus with a child. At these times we should neither blame our child for a bad attitude nor lay all the blame on the other party, but rather seek answers to the question, "What would Jesus do in this situation?"

Handling Value Conflicts

These values of God's kingdom stand in sharp contrast to the values of our world. Early in life our children need to learn what it means to hold these values. For instance, I've heard some women shun the work our church does in the inner city, saying, "Going there is too depressing." Chances are that in childhood these women were never exposed to anyone much poorer than themselves. So they find such poverty threatening and disheartening. But they have forgotten that Jesus called the poor blessed (Lk 6:20).

How can we respond when our child comes home from playing with someone who has neither toys nor new clothes and we are asked, "Why is Rose so poor? Doesn't Jesus love her?" This is our opportunity as parents to explain that while all we have comes from God and we give thanks for it, not receiving something is not a sign of God's disapproval or lack of love. We live in a world of sin where many people lack what they need, not because God doesn't care, but because of the selfishness of other people.

We learned this invaluable lesson as children in a concentration camp. While other prisoners blamed God for all the things that had happened to us, we as Christians recognized the reality of evil and humanity's freedom of choice. We knew that it was not God who had cooked up this prison camp. We also learned that when people make bad choices that hurt others, God is there to invade the evil situation and use bad for good purposes for those who love God (Rom 8:28).

When I had my own children, I was glad that they, too, were in a situation that forced them to face the conflict of good and evil. In the Philippines, they soon learned that in many areas the land was rich enough to provide plenty of food for everyone. But poor people went hungry when they were forced to move from their land by people more rich and powerful than themselves.

When landlords demanded an unfair portion of the crops from their tenant farmers, not enough food was left for the family that tilled the land. When our children were not more than eight or nine years old, they joined discussions with us about how there will be no more injustice in the City of God. Then those who have suffered in life like Lazarus, who begged at the gate of the rich man, will themselves be rich (Lk 16:19-31).

Any time we can discuss such conflicts of values with our children we are giving them the greatest preparation for life. Perhaps a TV newscast or documentary with starving children can offer us the concrete situation in which to discuss Lazarus' story or the meaning of the Beatitudes. If those children on the screen are hungry today, God will make it up to them some day. Justice will win. If that child is crying now, there will be laughter and joy ahead with God.

But that does not mean we should not do anything to relieve that child's hunger now. The Lord gave the story of the Good Samaritan to show us how to help the oppressed (Lk 10:25-37). As we share with our children the responsibility to do something about the suffering in the world, perhaps they will want to give what they have—50¢, $1, $5 or $10 saved up from their allowances. It's not the size of the gift, but the heart involvement which counts.

The great value of such an experience is that our children are getting involved in suffering to the point of making a small sacrifice and having their usual poverty-free world disturbed. We may as well let them know right now as children that the balance will tip in favor of the suffering poor some day, and the rich and well-fed will lose out.

When we talk about suffering with our children we must make it clear that suffering comes from the battle between good and evil, evil that Christ has overcome. And we can teach them that sin comes in many forms: in us, in the world, and in the devil.

Sin in Us

While each of us was created in the image of God with something Godlike in our nature, we have also been marred by sin. Therefore we have death and life struggling inside of us. Only as we are willing to die to the principle of sin in us can God break through and bring new life. It's a constant cycle of life and death—winter and spring.

Hence, we need to teach our children that if they steal money, cookies or anything else that is not theirs, they have to die to that sin by asking God and parents for forgiveness, by making restitution, and by forgiving themselves for their sin. They need to come to see that the self that caused the theft is contaminated with evil and needs to die. That principle of sin in each of us must be killed by dying: "We know that our old self was crucified with him so that the sinful body might be destroyed, and we might no longer be enslaved to sin. . . . So you also must consider yourselves dead to sin and alive to God in Christ Jesus" (Rom 6:6, 11).

Some will say that such thinking is too morbid for children. But should they be allowed to live in a make-believe world of goodness and painlessness when the real world is so different? Then what will they do when the effects of sin touch them? How much better to learn early the meaning of sin and grace. As children we used to sing:

I'm not too young to sin,
I'm not too young to die,
I'm not too little to begin
A life of faith and joy.

Jesus, I love Thy Name:
From evil set me free,
And ever keep Thy little lamb,
Who puts his trust in Thee.[1]

With teen-agers this message of sin and grace comes across even more readily—as parents and children sin against each other. For us with our children, reconciliation came at times only through deep suffering. Both sides had to be willing for self- crucifixion as we realized what had happened in our relationship.

Brother Bruno of the Search Institute describes the experience:

Being a parent of an adolescent who is learning to let go involves dying to the old self in a concrete manner. Our Christian heritage illumines and transforms this experience. . . . It is the basic story of death which brings life. . . . The parents and child must gradually let fade and die old established and accepted routines of behavior. There is evolving a new individual in the adolescent, a new life growing toward responsible adulthood.[2]

And so the cycle of living and dying to sin continues, but always with the knowledge that through Jesus life and goodness will always triumph in the end.

Sin in the World

Perhaps the way in which today's children face sin in the world most harshly is in the pressure to conform. They try so hard to conform to their world that they may miss the message of Jesus. One important area of conformity is rock music. Teen-agers will assure their parents that they are only listening to the music, not the lyrics, but one concerned parent writes:

There's a strong confusion between love and sex; there's a preaching about the joy of escape through alcohol and sex. . . . Some groups hint of occult messages in their lyrics and on their album covers. Many of the punk rock and heavy metal groups insinuate frightening preoccupation with violence, especially violence against women.[3]

So should parents forbid all rock? The trouble with this approach is that it can suggest that evil is located in things outside, while indeed it is present in the heart of each of us (Rom 3:23). It gives the false security that if I stay away from rock, I am pure!

But isn't rock music used to worship the devil? Probably all sorts of music we enjoy might have been used at some time to worship the devil and at other times to worship God. All forms of art can be used for or against God. But sin is located in people.

"So what should I do about rock music in my home?" parents ask. First, I suggest buying the lyrics to the popular songs and discussing them with your children. What a great way to raise the issue of the conflict of values! Once we know a bit more about what's going on in the rock world, we can turn the dial when the words of a song are offensive. (But as members of another generation, let's be careful about letting the noise dictate our actions. Remember, noise is usually not sin!)

The next step is to explore Christian rock as an alternative. There are rock stars who sing the Gospel message. Some of these groups and individuals lead exemplary lives and are held accountable by their churches. They may look like the teen subculture, but they are doing violence against sin when they believe things like this:

"Love not the world"—man, that is not an easy task. Because to be a friend of the world is to be an enemy of God. So we have to rebel against the value system that the world has. We have to question everything. We have to compare everything to Scripture. We are rebellious against sin. We are rebellious against the secular music industry.[4]

Keith Green was a singer popular with the younger generation, though he never went into hard rock. His music has led thousands to worship God "in spirit and in truth." We sang the simple lyrics of his beautiful chorus in Nairobi in an African home with an Indian Christian eager to learn the words:

O Lord, you're beautiful,
Your face is all I seek.
And when your eyes are on this child,
Your grace abounds to me.[5]

But there are not many Keith Greens. And there are many Christians disturbed over the influence of rock. Many of them tell me that there is something demonic about the music, not just the words. Since I have not studied this subject thoroughly, I do not want to pose as an authority, but rather present both sides of the issue.

For many years, I have had great admiration for Mother Basilea Schlink. We visited her Sisterhood of Mary once in Darmstadt, Germany, and attended her Bible lectures. While I do not necessarily agree with her, I think that her words on this topic deserve a hearing here:

Those who claim that no music is intrinsically evil, that music is a neutral force, are deluded. I Samuel 16:23 tells us that David sang and played his harp "inspired by the Spirit of God.". . . Music is always inspired by a spirit. . . . In the final analysis, it is not the lyrics but the spirit behind the music that is decisive. In this regard the Devil has been an unqualified success. He lets our fine religious words stand as long as his spirit marks the decibel level and the beat. . . . Granted, there are different degrees of intensity in this modern music. A wide range of milder forms are practiced. There are borderline cases that are not of satanic origin.[6]

While we do not have to take any human voice as the last word on any subject, we need to be warned to be alert to the deception that is going on all around us. We also have to be careful of easy answers to any complex problem. Even Mother Basilea admits there is rock that is not of satanic origin. I think what we all agree on is that as Christians, young or old, we want to submit to God only, and live in rebellion against the evil one.

The Devil

Jesus was rebellious against the devil. Three times the clever serpent tried to tempt the God-man, using Scripture, and three times Jesus used the Word of God against him (Mt 4:1-11). We need to study these passages with our children and teach them early in life to do battle against the devil, using the sword of the Word of God.

In *Pilgrim's Progress* the devil is portrayed as a lion, just as the Bible says, "Your adversary the devil prowls around like a roaring lion, seeking some one to devour" (1 Pet 5:8). But God has put the lions on a short tether for the sake of the pilgrims. No lion can touch them if they stay on the narrow road leading to the City of God. But it's easy to stray from the Way and that's when the lions can hurt us.[7]

The world, the flesh and the devil—sin in us, in the world and through our adversary—is a useful triad when we try to help young people see why they made a wrong decision. Some blame all the wrong on themselves and may develop an unhealthy "I hate myself" complex. But the more common pattern is to blame another person or the devil: "Mary made me do it," or "It was the devil's fault." The trick is as old as the creation story where Adam blamed Eve for his sin, and Eve in turn blamed the serpent.

The truth is that not just the sin in me, or sin in the world, or the devil caused my mistake, but all three worked together to win the battle over my new nature. But I never fight alone against the three. I can count on the Triune God to work for me—as the El Shaddai of the Old Testament, as Jesus the great winner at the cross, and as the Comforter always ready to pour soothing oil into my battle wounds. Therefore I never need to lose the battle, for "if God is for us, who is against us? . . . No, in all these things we are more than conquerors through him who loved us" (Rom 8:31, 37).

To counteract the power of this world, I need to remember that I belong to another kingdom. This kingdom is seen on earth in the Christian community I am part of where we are accountable to God and each other. And since the home is a microcosm of the Christian community, this is where I'll first experience that kingdom. Ideally speaking, it's also in the home where the children learn to face sin in themselves and the world.

The news about how to overcome evil is the good news I pass on to my children and grandchildren. Naturally there are times when I wish I could spare them from the severity of the battle against evil. At those moments we need to look to the goal of our journey, the day when we shall reach the City of God. Some day there will be no more conflict of values. Our Lord will come and put all things right.

Few authors have captured the glory of the coming of God's kingdom better than has C. S. Lewis in *The Last Battle* of The Narnia Chronicles. His story is just what our children need to find hope for the future and encouragement in battle. Aslan came to the discouraged children and animals who faced the end of their world of Narnia:

Had not the great Lion Aslan created Narnia, making the stars shine there and grass grow and trees and animals thrive in beauty and joy? Where was Aslan when those who loved him fell before such contemptible agents and all that Narnia stood for was destroyed? . . . It almost seemed as though nothing existed but evil. . . . Yet now appeared evidence of Aslan's best plan of all, for the children . . . suddenly found themselves . . . surrounded by light and space and joy and dressed in splendid robes as kings and queens of Narnia. And now Aslan himself came to them, larger and more golden than ever, and showed them the last things of old Narnia and then displayed the new unshadowed Narnia into which he led them joyously as they all went higher up and farther in. He told them they were just beginning Chapter One of the final Great Story.[8]

8

OUR
EXTENDED
FAMILY

JESUS WAS BORN INTO AN EXTENDED family. Matthew and Luke went to the trouble of recording the genealogy of Joseph, Jesus' legal father. We don't know too much about Jesus' extended family, but we do know that they traveled together on the annual pilgrimage to Jerusalem for the Passover. Why else, when their twelve-year-old boy was lost, did Mary and Joseph not miss Jesus till they had gone a day's journey and sought him among their kinsfolk? It was probably normal then—as it is now—for cousins of the same age to stick together whenever the families were joined (Lk 2:41-45).

Mary also appreciated the support of her extended family. First, when she needed someone to talk to about her unusual pregnancy, she went to the hill country and spent three months with her cousin Elizabeth (Lk 1:39-56). And when she stood at the foot of the cross and watched her son die family members stood by her (Jn 19:25-27).

The extended family has been part of our history from the earliest days until now. It's a universal reality. Everyone has an extended family. Everyone does not necessarily have a spouse, a child or siblings, but everyone belongs to a family with a father and mother who in turn had a father and mother— all the way back to Eden! Since the extended family is such a common denominator for the human race, it's interesting to ponder what unique role it has played in the history of the world. But perhaps an even more important question for us is what it can do for us in the future. What specific contributions can the extended family make toward the goal of restoring family life?

I think the extended family makes at least three important contributions. First, the extended family can be used of God to model the Christian life from generation to generation. Second, the nuclear family or single adult finds sustenance in the larger branch of the family tree. And third, the extended family can pick up the pieces of a broken marriage and be a reservoir of healing and strength for the survivors—the single parents and their children.

The gospel can turn the "black death" of divorce into a blessing for children who are surrounded by aunts, uncles and grandparents who can help fill the void left by a father or mother. We can picture the godly extended family as being united around a vision, like a dynasty of faith that goes on for generations.

The Faith of our Ancestors

"One generation shall laud thy works to another, and shall declare thy mighty acts," writes the psalmist (145:4). With the breakup of the extended family, we have lost this major way of making disciples and modeling the Christian life. When Paul wrote to Timothy he commented on how the young disciple had had the advantage of a godly mother and grandmother: "I am reminded of your sincere faith, a faith that dwelt first in your grandmother Lois and your

mother Eunice and now, I am sure, dwells in you. . . . From childhood you have been acquainted with the sacred writings which are
able to instruct you for salvation" (2 Tim 1:5; 3:15).

I thank God for women who have followed in Grandmother Lois's
footsteps. Some have chosen to babysit their grandchildren. Dr.
Miriam Adeney told me that she could never travel as she does to
missionaries around the world to share her insights on anthropol-
ogy if it were not for her mother's willingness to take care of the
children during her trips. And the children benefit from hearing of
the Christian faith from someone with an older perspective.

Not too long ago, I visited the home of a friend from China,
Winnie Englund Christensen. She and her husband bought a house
some years ago with an upstairs apartment for her retired missionary
parents. With them it was not so much for babysitting purposes as
to insure a good home for the old folks as long as possible, and a
close relationship between the three generations. I have heard the
children tell what a treat it has been for them to get to know their
grandparents in this way. Through modeling the torch has been
passed on to the third generation.

Aunts and uncles can also be a fine influence on children. But in
order for that to happen, parents must have healthy relationships
with their brothers and sisters. Nothing can poison these relationships quicker than family feuding, often over immaterial—or worse
yet—materialistic issues. I have known children who admired their
aunts and uncles as Christians, but were discouraged from spending
time with them by parents who had never been reconciled with
their siblings.

Each year our family attends the "Syttende mai" (Norwegian Con-
stitution Day) celebration in the Norwegian Lutheran Memorial
Church of Minneapolis. The Norwegian-American pastor there tells
how he was influenced as a child by those "giants of the earth"—
his uncles on Minnesota farms—who spoke few words but imparted
to him that the church and his personal relationship with God were
the most important factors in life. Those uncles sang both of old

Norway and of another Homeland to which they belonged.

Family Heritage

I am thankful for our family reunions where there has been no evidence of a generation gap. I can remember my daughter sitting with my brother, Edvard, both of them linguists, discussing morphemes by the hour. And Edvard's son, Finn, the third-generation missionary, talked missions with his Uncle Bob long into the night. What an honor when he chose his uncle as best man at his wedding!

As Bob and I pray for our children and grandchildren, we also pray for our nieces and nephews. I think of Edvard's daughter, Jean Valborg, who carries my mother's name, at Gordon-Conwell Seminary. She has brought us much joy as she has come to us for Christmas when her missionary parents have been overseas. When our youngest, O-i, got married, her sister and Jeanie were her attendants. What fun to see the three together who throughout childhood enjoyed brief holidays on the beaches of Taiwan, the Philippines, and Norway.

Another special contact with an uncle came when our daughter Kirsten and her pediatrician husband went to Thailand with Minnesota International Health Volunteers, the organization coordinated by my brother Hakon and founded by his pediatrician wife.

At the reunion hosted by my Norway-based brother Torje, I saw Hakon's wife, Karen, Torje's daughter, Hild, and her future husband, all sitting and discussing medicine, their profession. They were talking about health problems in the Third World. Concern for the oppressed is also part of our family heritage. My mother, a nurse, was a medical pioneer as she started the first clinic in her area of China—on the border of Mongolia—ten days from the nearest doctor.

We reminisced much about bygone days at that reunion—the first time we four Norwegian-Chinese siblings and our four spouses have ever been together. The last of the four couples to get married celebrated their twentieth wedding anniversary during that time. As the eight of us walked to the local Lutheran parish church and filled a long pew, we remembered our Christian family who for generations past have worshiped together. I wonder if they, too, claimed the promises I have claimed for my children, nephews and nieces:

I will pour my Spirit upon your descendants,
And my blessing on your offspring.
They shall spring up like grass amid waters,
like willows by flowing streams.
This one will say, "I am the LORD's"...
And another will write on his hand, "The LORD's." (Is 44:3-5)

On one of our trips to Norway I was lining up dates for the family to visit a first cousin, a second cousin and a third cousin. A concerned friend thought we were trying to pack too much into our short stay in Oslo. But when I explained to her that the three cousins were role models for our children, then she understood. If God has placed role models in our families, then we need to expose our children to them. Such relationships are worth more than many trips to Disneyland.

But in the Philippines, they don't stop with third cousins. The joke goes that they know their cousins all the way to the thirty-third degree. And while we in the West tend to ignore our poor relatives, Filipinos take rather seriously the instruction: "If any one does not provide for his relatives . . . he has disowned the faith and is worse than an unbeliever" (1 Tim 5:8). Cousins always know they are welcome at the table unannounced, even among those who have very little to share. Because of the frequent visiting back and forth, the result among Christians is that the older members become models of Christian faith and generosity to the younger.

But not everyone is ready for such close ties. One of the greatest fears of close family relationships in America is the threat of in-laws. Mother-in-laws have been the butt of both cruel and comical jokes for centuries. But I have been privileged to meet a few young women who have told me they became Christians because of their mother-in-laws.

In the Old Testament we also find such a story. Naomi lost her husband and two married sons in Moab where they went to get food during a famine in Judah. But when Naomi is ready to return to her own country and to say good-bye to her two Moabite daughters-in-law, she is surprised by one daughter-in-law, Ruth. Something about Naomi's faith must have caught Ruth's attention, for she refused to leave her mother-in-law. She pleads with Naomi: "Entreat me not to leave you or to return from following you; for where you go I will go, and where you lodge I will lodge; your people shall be my people, and your God my God" (Ruth 1:16).

This is a beautiful illustration of an older woman discipling a younger woman. There is a sense in which the Christian faith will keep our extended families strong, while the family will be the vehicle used of God to pass on the faith to the next generation.

Protecting the Nuclear Family

In addition to passing on the faith, the extended family can become a source of strength that will keep the nuclear family from disintegrating. When we deal with the tiny unit of mother, father and child, we need to see it as part of the whole family tree where the larger branches bring nourishment to the tiny twig. But why has this role of the extended family been overlooked?

In defense of the extended family, Parker J. Palmer writes:

For some of us, the community to build is the family, that ancient unit of common life which has been much-maligned in modern thought. . . . We must weigh the chances of family life against the economic aspirations which have contributed to the family's failure. For decades the family has been torn apart by our own desires for personal advancement. We have weakened and even destroyed the family by opting for personal mobility and economic success. We will rebuild community in the family only if the lure of achievement can take second place to the cultivation of relations between the generations.[1]

This problem came home to us when a young family, whose parents on both sides we have known for decades, wished to stay in Minnesota so their children could be close to their two godly sets of grandparents. But the 3M Company said that if the young father wanted to move up the economic ladder he had to be willing to move.

Such moves are made on the basis of the world's lie that the more we have, the happier and better we will be. After all, we owe it to our children to give them all that this world has to offer. But often the ones who need the extended family most are the ones who move away. Sometimes when husband and wife relationships are shaky, the couple thinks a new environment will heal their wounds. A better job and a bigger house are exchanged for the timeless support of extended family.

The church often further muddies the waters of such a shaky value system. It is interesting to see how when a worldly trend like materialism enters the church, the church tends to build a weak, defensive theology to justify it. Many of us need permission to sin—only a few sin boldly without permission—so what better place to get the permit to sin than the church? The church has to find Scriptures to prove that riches always come from God. And if all riches come from God, then surely it must be God's will to move to get more riches. But when we start with a false premise, of course we'll end up with a wrong conclusion.

Instead of leaving our families to get rich, I believe God is calling us to make great investments in each other—investments of time, money and emotional energy in order to keep the generations together. Genuine family togetherness will only come through conflict—as we work through our differences and separate true values from false ones. And the nuclear family will learn how to work through problems, not in isolation, but as part of a larger group. In both cases the cost will be time and tears, energy and privacy, cuts in salary and many other conveniences. Family community is born in the middle of conflict that is faced with Christian answers and values.

Protecting Single Members

"My family is always scolding me for having chosen the single life," my good friend Annie confided. "They seem to be obsessed with the fear that some day they'll have to take care of me when I'm too old to take care of myself."

Such cruel treatment is so out of place, especially in a Christian family. Her married brothers and sisters might be left alone by their spouses, and Annie will be the one to take care of them. That's what happened to Mabel, a beautiful Christian single woman who lives in our town. She moved in with her widowed sister-in-law who had cancer and stayed with her till she died.

Interdependence in the family means we are there for whoever needs us—the ones who are single by choice like Annie and Mabel, or those who lose their spouse through death, desertion or divorce. To complicate matters many who are unmarried by circumstance are single parents as well and need role models for their children. Whichever category the single person belongs to, there is a need for a close community, and what more natural Christian community to surround the single parent than the person's own extended family?

But it is a sad fact that many singles find community neither in the church nor the family. This in turn leads to bad marriages. When I ask women who come to tell me of their oppressive marriages how they got into such a mess, the common answer is, "Because I was lonely."

I asked the same question of a lesbian and got the same answer. People will go to extremes to alleviate loneliness. My advice to young Christians who are lonely like this is either to find a Christian community and get involved or to look for community within their extended families. Christian extended families must open their hearts and homes to take in their single relatives. And singles must give as well as receive hospitality from the rest of their families.

"It isn't good . . . to be alone," was one of God's earliest proclamations at the dawn of human history (Gen 2:18 Living Bible). God's intention has never been that people should be lonely. The popular poem tells the truth, "No man is an island." Singleness is not bad, but loneliness can be devastating. Jesus and Paul showed us by both personal example and their teachings that it can be normal and fulfilling to be single (Mt 19:10-12; 1 Cor 7:25, 40). But both of them promoted Christian community and were seldom alone.

Another interesting factor about Jesus and Paul is that their circle of friends and coworkers included both men and women. Jesus traveled with women companions as well as his twelve disciples (Lk 8:1-3; Mt 27:55-56), and Paul sent greetings in Romans 16 to many men as well as ten women with whom he had a close relationship. If we look on Jesus and Paul as role models for singles, this suggests that the Christian community they choose should include both men and women.

Therefore, while not everyone will be married, all will live as male and female and appreciate the spiritual, intellectual and psychological fellowship that exists between men and women created in the image of God. This truth has tremendous implications for singles who in our sex-crazy society and marriage-centered churches so often feel like second-class people. Only as we widen the family circle to include the extended family can we make room for singles to function in a healthy Christian environment as males and females in fellowship with one another. This fits into God's original plan that no man or woman should be lonely.

The lines of loving communication always need to be kept open between single and married members. If one side blames the other for snobbishness, the family will never be reconciled. The squabbles that take place between husband and wife are merely reflections of the squabbles that so often mar the harmony in the extended family.

During times of family tension it is easy for a single person to want to bail out and take a good job across the country. "After all,

I have my own life to live," the argument goes. Perhaps a salary raise is all that's needed to tip the decision in favor of moving away. For a Christian single this often means invading new territory where their standards of chastity will not be understood. Old or young, married or single, we all need community in order to be true to our commitment.

Picking up the Pieces of the Broken Family

Singleness comes to some through death, desertion or divorce. When this happens, the extended family ought to respond.

On one of my speaking tours I stayed with a family whose house has become a home to me over the years, and of course I caught up on the news. The daughter, a single missionary, had arrived home seriously ill on a stretcher just about the time when the son's marriage was falling apart. Because of deep Christian roots in the soil of God's love, this family was able to absorb both problems at the same time. But what if the daughter had had no home to come home to? And what if the son had had no Christian family to turn to in his distress?

This is why our society is falling apart. People in distress have nowhere to turn unless they pay a counsellor forty or a hundred dollars an hour to listen to their heartaches. Some people need psychotherapy, and it can be beneficial because it helps a person work through problems on a regular basis. But most people just need family—perhaps family members who will sit with the person week after week and listen as the individual works through personal problems. Folk in traditional cultures are horrified when they hear that in the U.S. the brokenhearted have to pay someone to hear their sad story.

It is a sobering commentary on our society that often there is no Christian community to absorb a person's grief. So again we give the trumpet call for the Christian extended family to come to the aid of the men or women facing permanent separation from a spouse they had dreamed of living with for the rest of their lives.

111

I think of my own maternal grandmother who became a widow in her twenties. My grandfather was the captain of a large sailing ship. The ship was due into port for Christmas, and many excited families in Kristiansand were waiting for their husbands and fathers. They waited and waited for the ship, and then for news of the ship, but no news ever came. It was years later before the wreck of the ship was found.

"I loved him so much," my grandmother told me fifty years later when she could confide in me as an adult. She told me of the difficult times of being mother to three fatherless little children and how fortunate she was that she could stay home with her children and support them with her knitting machine. When an order was finished my mother was the delivery service who walked to the house of the customer with the knitted garment. My grandmother also told me of summers spent on her childhood farm as her parents poured out their love on the fatherless children. Truly God had been good to her since she lost her husband.

Her family tried to fulfill James's definition of true Christianity: "Religion that is pure and undefiled before God and the Father is this: to visit orphans and widows in their affliction, and to keep oneself unstained from the world" (1:27). The Bible has always had much to say about our responsibility to the widowed and fatherless (Ex 22:22; Deut 10:18; 14:29; 16:11, 14; 26:12; Ps 146:9; Is 1:17, 23).

Aid as Well as Comfort

But what did James mean by keeping oneself "unstained from the world"? The stain of the world could well be the three sources of sin that we've already discussed—money, sex and power. In the first century women and children without male protection could easily be abused physically, swindled out of their inheritance financially, and generally disenfranchised. That's why Jesus said, "Beware of the scribes . . . which devour widows' houses and for a shew make long prayers" (Lk 20:46-47 KJV). Today, as well as then, widowed and divorced family members need some very practical helps as well as a shoulder to cry on once in a while.

Far more single mothers than fathers live on incomes below the poverty line. When a woman is widowed or divorced and has children, she faces a number of significant issues. Money may be the biggest issue. In our discriminatory society, women still make substantially less money than men, even for equivalent jobs. And many married women have sacrificed career time and training in order to have children. So when they are left alone, they return to the work force at a great disadvantage. And they face the issue of how to nurture their children adequately and still work.

We have already discussed children's need for love and attention and nurturing, both during preschool years and later. If a single parent left alone with children cannot be present during important times, the extended family should step in to help, or in absence of extended family, the church community.

In a sense, single parents are the new "widows" from a biblical standpoint. But our modern "widows" are neediest at a much earlier age—when their children are young. They need help to raise them as Christians. Could we imagine Stephen, the martyr, "a man full of faith and of the Holy Spirit," just doling out the food for the widows and not caring about their spiritual welfare (Acts 6)?

Single parents today need from the extended Christian family, or the church community, role models for their children so they will see Christianity in action and not just hear about it at church. They also need help in getting whatever aid is available for them from the government. If this help is insufficient, single parents need financial assistance from either the extended family or the church so they can stay home with their small children and be sure their schoolchildren are cared for during out-of-school hours.

In the letter to Timothy, Paul puts the responsibility for widows first on the shoulders of the extended family. If there was no family around, the church had to take over: "If a widow has children or grandchildren, let them first learn their religious duty to their own family and make some return to their parents; for this is acceptable in the sight of God. . . . If any one does not provide for his relatives, and especially for his own family, he has disowned the faith and is worse than an unbeliever. . . . If any believing woman has relatives who are widows, let her assist them; let the church not be burdened, so that it may assist those who are real widows" (1 Tim 5:4, 8, 16).

Today the older widows Paul is talking of are at least partly taken care of by pensions and social security. Since the "widows" of our time include young mothers and fathers with children, we have to think of parents taking care of their children and grandchildren, rather than just as the text suggests, children and grandchildren helping the older generation. The details have changed, but not the principles of the unchanging Word of God. We are still called upon to make financial sacrifices on the basis of unconditional love.

This means that an extended Christian family can either help financially so the single parent does not have to work, or they can provide an apartment next door or upstairs, so that there can be help with the children when the single parent has to work. As Paul suggested, if there is no family available, the church should take on this responsibility.

The biggest problem today when such a suggestion is made is the fear that people have of being used. Parents of single parents, and grandparents of motherless and fatherless children, have a holy fear of their children taking advantage of them. What if they make huge financial sacrifices, plus giving up their privacy and plans for a care-free retirement, and the loving gift is not fully appreciated?

That's always the risk we take with unconditional love. Jesus took the same risk when he ended up weeping over the Jerusalem that rejected his love. In the final analysis, we have to look at our commitment to our family as a commitment to God. If the family we sacrificed for does not appreciate what we have done, Jesus does. He receives it as an offering of love, for "as you did it to one of the least of these my brethren, you did it to me" (Mt 25:40).

As the Cursillo song goes:

Have you ever stood in the family

With the Lord there in your midst,
Seen the face of Christ on your neighbor?
Then I say you've seen Jesus my Lord.[2]

Besides help with their children, singles need help in dealing with their guilt. While my grandmother in her deep sorrow knew she had no part in the storm on the North Sea that caused my grandfather's death, the divorced spouse usually lives with guilt that maybe the marital storm could somehow have been avoided.

Divorce is always a messy business because it is sin. But just as King David found forgiveness for his sins of murder and adultery, so the person who has experienced divorce can find forgiveness today. Divorce is not an unpardonable sin. There is forgiveness and healing also for this sin. None of us are accepted by God because we are good, but only because we are forgiven. Often in the bosom of the loving extended family this message of complete forgiveness is best communicated.

A Christian Dynasty

Christian families can become holy beacons for all those around them. When several generations are Christians, the family takes on the ethos of a "holy nation." Such can be the goal for every Christian—to make his or her family into a holy nation. We can begin by thanking God for each family member who is a believer, and we can work toward reconciliation and Christian community among those who are already on the pilgrimage.

Next, we can reach out in love to those who are not Christians and keep the lines of loving communication open.

Third, if someone is the first Christian in the family, that person can start praying that a Christian dynasty will grow like the sands on the seashore from one believer. This is what happened to Abraham: "By faith he sojourned in the land of promise, as in a foreign land, living in tents. . . . For he looked forward to the city which has foundations, whose builder and maker is God. . . . Therefore from one man, and him as good as dead, were born descendants as many as the stars of heaven and as the innumerable grains of sand by the seashore" (Heb 11:9-10, 12).

P. J. Malcolm was a man of faith like Abraham—Bob's grandfather who came from Sweden over a hundred years ago and bought the farm on which we now live. He and Grandma Christina became the spiritual leaders in this community as settlers came from miles around to their home for singing, prayer and Bible study. The outreach was the natural overflow of love of a Christian family for others around them. When any Swede was in trouble, Grandpa would sell some land and help him out, so that's how the land was shrunk, but what a legacy! Little did they know back in the 1870s that they were starting a little Christian dynasty on this hill.

We are living on holy ground as I think of all the singing and Gospel proclamation that has taken place on this land. Everyone who remembers old Grandpa P. J. tells us that nobody ever saw him angry. Though struggling with all the impossible odds of a typical Swedish immigrant, Grandpa is always remembered walking up this hill, singing the songs of Zion.

When Bob and I returned from our fifteen years in the Philippines, we were given a lot by Bob's folks on this farm. The first year here Bob built the house we now live in with his own hands, in the old Swedish tradition. We were glad for the years our children had the opportunity to get to know their grandparents after the years abroad. Until Grandma and Grandpa reached the City of God a few years ago, we were three generations living in three separate households on this family farm.

This was also our opportunity to learn about love and forgiveness as we attempted to live as a Christian family community. One of our early experiences happened when my sister-in-law started a neighborhood prayer group in her house—in the tradition of all the other meetings that have been held in homes on this hill. But I thought we should join a larger group that met a couple of miles away. After I suggested this to the women, our small group broke up. When I realized not all wanted to join the larger group, I saw that I had been out of order in suggesting what the group should do. I had to confess to my sister-in-law my sin of wanting to control the group. We read together this Scripture: "The Lord Jesus on the night in which he was betrayed took bread, and when he had given thanks, he broke it, and said, 'This is my body which is for you' " (1 Cor 11:23-24).

In the midst of betrayal, community was born between Jesus and his disciples. There was love and forgiveness. And that's what happened to us as two sisters-in-law. Together with our husbands and children and grandparents we were discovering love and forgiveness as we began to experience family community on the pilgrimage. It meant learning to walk in step with the Savior and each other.

9

REACHING BEYOND THE HOME

Apackage of tea bags arrived safely from the U.S. for a missionary family at their headquarters in Mexico City.

"But they're used!" cried eight-year-old Tommy as he scrutinized the carton of sad-looking brownish gauze bags. They were stuffed together like a pile of dead mice, their thin tails stapled to name tags. "This one's called Black Cat," Tommy continued as he tried to unloose his victim by the tail. Tommy's mother was busy studying the return address on the box.

"Bless their hearts," she mumbled to herself. "It's First Church again. Guess after four years in Mexico they thought used tea bags would do." Like Tommy's parents, missionaries do open some strange parcels from home. That's because many Christians have an inaccurate view of missions. Somehow once a missionary has moved far away to that unknown place "out there on the field," everything must have changed, including his normal taste for unused tea bags!

Usually, however, the most insulting hand-me-downs are reserved not for the missionaries, but for the "natives." Some of the old clothing sent to the mission field makes excellent costumes for skits at conferences. One skit in the Philippines featured a well-built muscular male missionary in ladies' high heels and a holey black lace dress.

"Oh, you can send any old stuff to those natives over there," I overheard a matronly voice tell her companion in the pew. "They're so poor, they're glad for anything." By sending our castaways to people we do not know, in faraway places, are we not revealing a sense of racial and social superiority? It's time to sound the prophetic word about our sense of belonging to the family of God around the world.

Where World Consciousness Begins

The place for such a global vision of God's household to grip us is in the Christian family. There children can learn early in life to treat other races as part of the family of God.

The early church certainly had a world consciousness and an international flavor starting with the day of Pentecost. How has our modern church lost it? And how can we regain it? I believe we lost it first when the church moved out of the home and became institutionalized. Then families stopped thinking of themselves as a microcosm of the church.

Because world consciousness was first lost in the family, that is where it has to be regained. Christian offspring are produced in the family, and that's the most natural place for the sharing of our faith with others. That's where the hurting people of the world will come first for healing, before they go to the church. The Christian family is also the arena where new missionaries are made, and where Christianity will be kept alive during wars and chaos and persecution. We will look in this chapter at what it means for the Christian family to be a microcosm of the church.

We have seen in earlier chapters how Christian families are perpetuated as older Christians model a holy life before the children. Part of that modeling includes concern for a lost and hurting world. Children are never too young to learn that they belong to all races and everyone they meet deserves to know the good news, "Jesus loves me." In fact, it's the family committed to such a goal of reaching others with God's love who will survive, rather than the family that concentrates on its own survival. "For whoever would save his [family] will lose it, and whoever loses his [family] for my sake will find it" (Mt 16:25, my changes).

With the breakdown of the family in the West, much has been said about putting the family first. But as Christians we are called to put first Jesus and his compassion for the harassed and helpless people around the world (Mt 9:36-38). When the family prays for and befriends a hurting world, the home is doubly blessed: by hospitality shown to strangers (who might turn out to be angels—Heb 13:2!), and by our own children who come to faith in such an environment of love and sharing.

Raising New Converts

"What do you say to all those people who come to you and tell you all their problems?" came the surprising question from my eight-year-old O-i. When we were in the Philippines I used to listen to the stories of those in distress. I could see she was curious about this.

"Basically, after I've listened a long time, I tell them I'm as human as they are and therefore can't do much about the problem. But we have One who cares for us and can do something about impossible situations, so I suggest that together we give the problem to Jesus. Then in faith we wait for an answer," I told her, simplifying things a little and expecting that to be the end of the subject. But during the summer holidays O-i asked if she could play receptionist for me—greeting people at the door, inviting them in for Kool-Aid, and talking to them till I was ready to see them. Sounded like a wonderful idea!

One day the long, sad story I was listening to took longer than usual and I was getting a bit nervous about O-i having entertained a woman in the living room for over an hour. I didn't want to wear out her enthusiasm. Finally my session came to an end and I entered the living room a bit flushed and full of apologies to the woman I had kept waiting for so long.

"It's all right," she said with a happy laugh. "You see, your little girl has told me to give my problem to Jesus. She said you really can't help me. It's only Jesus who can, so I've given my problem to him." She was so relaxed and full of smiles that I could see that she had been relieved of her burden and certainly was in no mood to cough up all her problems again just to be polite. So we had another glass of Kool-Aid together, a friendly chat, and she was on her way, rejoicing in God's goodness.

To me what O-i had done was not only cute. It was a tremendous affirmation to me that I was on the right track. For years I'd struggled with the balance between family and ministry. I lived under a certain false guilt that if my children didn't love the Lord, it would be because I had ministered to others and neglected them. I had sat under a lot of teaching that warned young mothers not to be too involved in ministry.

It was presented as an either/or proposition. Either you would have a godly family, or you would have a ministry outside the home. You had to choose. Yet with my China Inland Mission background where every woman, married or single, was a full-time missionary, I also felt guilty if I didn't minister to the Filipinos we had come to serve.

So this was a struggle I constantly gave to God, praying that I wouldn't go too far in either direction. Through the example of dedicated older Filipino women who had much larger families than I had as well as much larger ministries, I gradually came to see that it did not have to be either family or ministry. God can use all of us, men and women, to minister to our own children as well as those beyond the home "for the promise is to you and to your children and to all that are far off" (Acts 2:39).

The women who became my models also thought in terms of seasons of life when they might be more involved outside the home than other times. When their children were toddlers, people could come to their homes to see them. Later when the children were in school all day, these women were free to go out to evangelize. And when they reached the empty-nest stage, some of the grandmothers were out evangelizing all the time.

The Filipino women were also models in their willingness to open their homes to strangers, while in the West we worry about having our privacy invaded. What an affirmation O-i's first counselling adventure was to me that a home-centered ministry could lead my children closer to the Lord and the people for whom he died, and not away from the Lord.

Of course there were the times, too, when there were complaints that Ma was too busy. When I was at the employment center that I helped to start for a population of a million people without one, the children would phone and my good friend Alyce Pedraya would tell them that I was in a very important meeting. "But she's our mother and her first responsibility is to us," they would tell Alyce. I was glad they felt free to say so rather than inwardly harboring a sense of rejection.

Through all such adjustments, I am grateful that our children learned to love the Lord early in life. Michael Green writes in *Evangelism in the Early Church*:

> It is clear that children can partake in the kingdom of heaven, that their attitude of trusting obedience is in fact a model for adults to follow if they are to gain eternal life (Mt 18:2-4). . . . It is through the witness and example of the Christian home that children are brought into and nourished within the fellowship.[1]

Green goes on to cite many early martyrs who came from Christian homes. When Justin went to his early death around A.D.165, Paeon and Euelpistus were martyred with him. When the prefect asked Paeon where he learned his Christianity, he answered, "From our parents we received this good confession"— which cost him his life. And Euelpistus answered, "I willingly heard the words of Justin. But from my parents too I learned to be a Christian." Justin Martyr, on the other hand, came from a pagan home, but tells us that "many men and women of the age of sixty and seventy years have been disciples of Christ from childhood." Pliny said about Bithynia in A.D. 112 that there were many little children among the Christians as the new faith had ensnared "many of every age."[2]

Clement of Rome, too, wrote about what a Christian home should be: "Let our children partake of the training that is in Christ. Let them learn how humility avails with God, what pure love can do with him, how the fear of him is good and great and saves those who live therein in holiness and a pure mind."[3]

The Center for Evangelism
The famous Origen of Alexandria came from one of those strong Christian families who let their light shine during the Severan persecution. Eusebius writes: "Origen had even then [A.D. 202] made no little progress in the doctrine of faith as he had been conversant with the Holy Scriptures from a child. He had been considerably trained in them by his father." He also had a good mother—with a sense of humor. When the young Origen wanted to join his father in prison and be martyred with him, she hid her son's clothes![4]

Origen carried on the faith of his parents, converting many to belief in Christ, including Gregory, the son of an affluent pagan family in Pontus. Gregory and his brother Athendorus were on their way to Beirut to study rhetoric and law. Origen invited the two students into his home, and there they learned about Christ. Instead of continuing on their journey, they stayed for some time and developed a love for God. Gregory said of Origen:

He possessed a rare combination of a certain sweet grace and persuasiveness, along with a strange power and constraint. . . . The stimulus of friendship was also brought to bear on us—a stimulus not easily withstood, but keen and most effective—the argument of a kind and affectionate disposition. . . . And thus, like some spark lighting upon our inmost soul, love was kindled and burst into flame within us—a love to the Holy Word, the most lovely object of all, who attracts all irresistibly towards himself by his unutterable beauty."[5]

Gregory went on to become a missionary bishop who was instrumental in bringing many in Pontus to faith in Christ Jesus.

The important part of Origen's story is that he welcomed the young men into his home. What more natural place than the home for inviting someone else to join the journey to the City of God? We don't know how long Gregory and his brother stayed, but the home atmosphere made the prolonged visit they needed possible. Homes like Origen's were lights in the darkness for those who needed the gospel. It was the tradition started by Paul and the other apostles in Acts where most of the activity takes place in homes.

Many centuries later, Richard Baxter rediscovered this fact for himself when he began conducting meetings in homes for the purpose of evangelism:

After years of faithful preaching, Richard Baxter turned to house meetings, giving Monday and Tuesday entirely to this work, from morning to night 'taking about fifteen or sixteen families in a week, that we may go through the parish, in which there are upwards of 800 families, in the year. I cannot say yet that one family hath refused to come to me. . . . And I find more outward signs of success with most that do come than from all my public preaching to them.' "[6]

But Baxter lived at a time when the English people were a homogeneous group. Today small groups in homes sometimes have a rough time making it because of the diversity within our society which makes it difficult to fellowship together with ease. We have to deal with racial and economic differences. But where segregation exists and persists in churches, schools and neighborhoods, families have a unique power to effect social change.

These changes will occur, not because of some idealistic egalitarianism, but only as the gospel is preached as the "saving power of God for everyone who has faith—the Jew first, but the Greek also—because here is revealed God's way of righting wrong" (Rom 1:16 NEB). And there is much that is wrong that needs to be righted.

A beautiful friend from Africa was with me when I went to speak in another city. We were welcomed into the home of wonderful, warm Christians where we were having our dinner before the evening meeting. My friend played with the two-year-old while his mother was busy in the kitchen. As this African woman held out her hand to him, the little boy said, "Dirty, dirty!" Probably he had never had a black person reach out to him before. His response showed a distressing lack of familiarity with people of other races. If that continues, it might grow into adult prejudice born of ignorance. One of the great gifts we can give our children from the start is friendship with people from all different races, countries and walks of life.

While we don't have apartheid in our government, like South Africa does, we have vestiges of racism in home and church. This is one of the greatest hindrances to missions today. God in his sovereign will has brought the world to our doorstep. We don't have to travel across the sea to meet strangers as in bygone days. But because of the prejudice that keeps Christians from opening their homes to other races, along with the excuses that we are too busy making a living and taking care of our own, we miss the high calling.

Every home can become a microcosm of the church. "It is through the preaching of the gospel by humble folk who do not advertise themselves but confidently proclaim the Lordship of Jesus, that God's light breaks into blinded hearts," says Michael Green. "Now if you believe that outside of Christ there is no hope, it is impossible to possess an atom of human love and kindness without being gripped with a great desire to bring men to this . . . salvation."[7] When you have a home you need no other podium or stadium for such concern to be demonstrated. And in the process of showing hospitality, the needs of the whole person will be discovered—if there are wounds that need healing or questions that need answering.

Healing the Wounded

Jesus tells us what to do about these wounded people in his cross-cultural story of the helpful Samaritan and the wounded Jew (Lk 10:29-37). The Jew was hurt by violent robbers and left half-dead on the side of the road. The same has happened to millions today. There are so many wounded by the wayside as we make our pilgrimage that we are all tempted to look the other way, like the priest and Levite did. Yet the hero of the story is not another priest, but a businessman from another nation. Jesus' final twist in the story is bringing in a rescuer from the despised nation to help the man from the respectable nation.

What is Jesus trying to tell us? Jesus was telling people they didn't have to be religious leaders in order to act with compassion. Every home can become a place of rescue for wounded travelers. For instance, our good friends, Bonnie and John DeJong, have over the years had a constant stream of people with various needs stay in their home. When we visited their house the first time we met a woman who had left her husband. Bonnie didn't talk to her about it. She just gave her a loving atmosphere for her wounds to heal. And she answered the woman's questions. For years now this woman and her husband have been reunited and serving the Lord together. And now they have an open home for other wounded travelers.

When South-East Asian refugee children needed a place to go the day they arrived—until a regular family could be found—again the De Jongs opened their home. It was delightful to see them each Sunday with their huge family of Asian children. In the last couple of years they have adopted several abused children so that with their own two, plus the adopted ones, they now have ten. Like the Good

Samaritan, John is an insurance salesman and Bonnie a former airline stewardess. They have entered into the fellowship of Jesus' suffering as they have taken on the wounds of afflicted children and sought to right the wrong through the gospel (Phil 3:10; Rom 1:16 NEB).

Homemade Missionaries

The homes that reach out to the wounded are often the ones that produce the best future missionaries. I believe when a child grows up sensitized not only to the needs of family members, but to what's going on elsewhere, that child has a head start no educational institution can give.

I received a welcome letter some years ago from my friend Raquel in the Philippines. It is one of those letters I'll keep because it tells of her daughter, my namesake, at age three:

She is beginning to help us in our ministry. She's always with us every time we have our Bible study at the Detention Center. She usually sings during sing-along time before we start. . . . Besides entertaining prisoners with her songs, she entertains them with her stories. She really can talk to people. You know, before sleeping we pray together and if I say Amen without including the indigents, she asks me right away, "Why didn't you pray for the indigents and the prisoners?" So we have to pray again and include them in our prayer. I thank and praise God for her.

The Bible tells us to "train up a child in the way he should go, and when he is old he will not depart from it" (Prov 22:6). If we start them early with concern for the poor and prisoners, when they are old they will remember this. On the other hand, if we start them on the road of selfishness that's the road they'll take when they get older.

I've enjoyed watching my nieces next door share their toys, books and bicycles with the Hmong children who lived across the street. As newcomers these children were not used to American toys. One girl in particular would spend hours in one of the rooms inspecting old and new toys. Sometimes the children would be all over the house. What marvelous training in crosscultural friendship. When the Hmong family moved to California, the Van Schootens went West for their vacation and the highlight of the trip for the girls was visiting their Hmong friends. It even beat Disneyland! We wouldn't be surprised if a missionary or two comes out of such a home.

The only place where the attitude toward people from other races is going to change is in the home. Thank God for homes that have taken in foreign students as members of the family, written regularly to them when they return to their homelands, and later visited them. Children from such homes are rich spiritually compared to those who have never had a foreigner eat at their table.

The Mitchells are such a family that trained their children with world awareness from the start. The result was that five out of the six children went to the mission field—to Indonesia, India, Japan, Hongkong, Ethiopia, Kenya, and Trinidad. The sixth one helped his parents with the mission board they founded. The father of the six used to say, "The only thing we can bring to heaven with us is our children." We had the privilege of learning from the Mitchells and of knowing three of their children. Now it is their grandchildren that are the missionaries.

I was talking to a grandmother visiting her family in our church about the possibility of her son's taking a short-term assignment overseas with his wife and children. "I think they must wait till the children are grown," she said.

"Oh no," I answered. "The children would be gypped. They would lose the greatest experience of their life—living in a foreign country for a couple of years." Taking children abroad for longer or shorter trips—or paying their way to visit a missionary friend—is a marvelous way of exposing them to missions. And then pray that they will be open to God's call whatever it might mean: having an open home for strangers in the U.S., going overseas as full-time missionaries, or going as tentmakers in the tradition of Paul.

Open Homes for Strangers and Outcasts

"How many of you are willing to share your mommy?" I asked to everyone's surprise at the Mother-Daughter Banquet where I was speaking. I paused to take a long look at the little girls in their pretty print dresses with their ponytails or short curls or bangs. Curiosity was mingled with fear in their bright eyes and sweet faces.

"You see, there are lots of little girls who don't have a mommy like yours to bring them to a nice banquet like this," I continued. "They have no mommies to hug and kiss them and ask them, 'How was school today?' Are you willing to share your mommy with these little girls? Can they come to your house for snacks after school?" By this time one or two shy hands went up in the front row, and I could see a few nods from the back. But from most of the girls and their mothers I only got puzzled looks. The concept of sharing their homes seemed foreign.

My brother Ed had a similar experience when he gave a missionary talk at the evening service in a church. With dramatic detail he told the story of the little boy who shared his lunch (Jn 6:8-13). Then he asked the children if they would be willing to share their lunches if they were given such a wonderful opportunity. "No," came the answer loud and clear from a little boy sitting with his family. Ed took it in his stride, acknowledging the boy's feelings and continuing the story. After the service, the little boy came up and put his arms around Ed's leg, saying, "I'll share my lunch."

For most people it takes longer for the principle of sharing to sink in. It just does not come easy to any of us—young or old—to share our parents, our lunch or our homes. When we open our homes and hearts to people, we are practicing the radical obedience Jesus called his followers to when he said,

When you give a lunch or dinner, do not invite your friends or your brothers or your relatives or your rich neighbors—for they will invite you back, and in this way you will be paid for what you did. When you give a feast, invite the poor, the crippled, the lame, and the blind; and you will be blessed, because they are not able to pay you back. God will repay you on the day the good people rise from death. (Lk 14:12-14 TEV)

I remember teasing my mother as a teen-ager when she had invited company: "I guess you are going to have some of your lame and halt and blind over." In this way she was teaching me that certain people you must go out of your way to invite. She had a different type of entertainment list than what the etiquette experts recommend. The people that will always be the most appreciative of our hospitality and the most open to the gospel are the hungry, the poor, the sick, the prisoners and the strangers. In Jesus' most profound sermon on the topic he says, "When I was a stranger you took me into your home" (Mt 25:31-46 NEB).

The Christian Family in the Future

We don't know what the future holds, or how long families in the West will have the freedom to plan trips around the world—or invasions into enemy territory with the gospel. But we do know what our Bible tells us:

You will be hated by all nations for my name's sake. And then many will fall away, and betray one another, and hate one another. And many false prophets will arise and lead many astray. And because wickedness is multiplied, most men's love will grow cold. But he who endures to the end will be saved. And this gospel of the kingdom will be preached throughout the whole world, as a testimony to all nations; and then the end will come. (Mt 24:9-14)

While we tend to think this preaching will be done by traditional missionary societies, this is unlikely since the official Western missionary presence is no longer welcome in many places in the world. The professional missionary movement that my family has been part of for three generations is on its way out. In the future world evangelism will be done two primary ways. First, by families and individuals who go incognito into a country hostile to Christianity and live there as a Christian presence, earning their own living and answering questions as people ask (1 Pet 3:15).

Second, world evangelization will be done through the means stressed all through this chapter—the open home for strangers from all countries. Whether a family has an open home where they are living now, or whether God wants them to move across the world, in either case each family of pilgrims will be like a missionary society in itself, chosen to be a light to the nations. So we have come full circle back—as in the early church—to the family unit as the center for the evangelization of the world.

This point was made at the Catholic Synod of the Family in 1980: "The bishops acknowledged that the family was not so much the object of evangelization, to be converted by the 'real church,' as the agent of evangelization, with members ministering to each other and to the world."[8]

Just as the family is the ideal unit into which our children are born with loving and caring parents, so the family is the ideal place for spiritual children to be born into the kingdom. In neither case is the job finished at birth. It's just beginning. Whether the spiritual children live with us or not, they need to have a home environment available to them to help them move from the wrong road of the old life to the new road of the pilgrim on the way to the City of God.

The journey to the City of God for families with a vision to reach the nations may take them through war-torn territory, but as long as the war is waged outside, and not inside the family, the children feel safe. The secret of their joy comes from obedience to the God who called them to be a light, first to their own in the nuclear and extended family, and then to the myriads of families beyond themselves.

As I look back on our experience as a missionary family in the Philippines during the fifteen years that both our children were home with us, I thank God for the vision God gave us. One of our special family ministries was visiting political prisoners, bringing them mosquito nets, cake, books, art supplies, and enjoying an afternoon of Bible study, singing and games. Our children ministered by trying to cheer up these kids—just a few years older than themselves—who often did not know why they were in prison.

Many of the political prisoners visited our home after they were released. Some had become Christians while in prison, and some not, but they were all welcome. We were also in touch with criminal prisoners. One of these was Pedro, who went to prison for manslaughter. We met him years afterwards as he wandered around like a hobo after having served his sentence. Nobody would believe his story of conversion enough to hire him. So Pedro took to the road. We were on his map as he walked from town to town. We expected a visit from Pedro about once a year.

I shall never forget when Pedro arrived and Bob was out of town. What should I do? Give him a bed in my house? The young coed living with us voted no. And a missionary friend told me I was crazy to consider letting an ex-murderer sleep in my house with "only helpless womenfolk."

But with Jesus' words, "When I was a stranger you took Me into your home," ringing in my ears, Pedro stayed. To refuse him would have been to refuse Jesus or to refuse one of those angels whom the Bible promises will visit us if we show hospitality to strangers (Heb 13:2-3).

I usually asked Pedro to recite Psalm 23 in his beautiful Cebuano when he came. With his sunburnt skin and face roughened by exposure to wind and rain, I thought, he sure looks like a shepherd. Then that night as he recited those beautiful words I thought—he sure looks like *the* Shepherd! The room was filled with awe as my children and I silently watched his every move and listened. Was Jesus the Shepherd at our table?

"When I was a stranger you took Me into your home."

10

JOURNEY'S
END

ABDUL IS A CHARMING YOUNG
Muslim who acknowledged Jesus Christ as his Lord and Savior a few
years ago. The most heartbreaking reaction from his family was an
official document from his father, made back in his homeland and
signed by a notary public. After telling me about it, Abdul read it
to me, holding back the tears as he did so. The document declared
that he was no longer a son in the family into which he was born.
He had been disowned!

Before I had time to let this tragedy sink into my soul, or dry my
tears, this young man, still holding the paper in his left hand, picked
up his New Testament and read this from his newfound Father:
"In my Father's house are many rooms; if it were not so, would I
have told you that I go to prepare a place for you? And when I go
and prepare a place for you, I will come again and will take you to

myself, that where I am you may be also" (Jn 14:2-3).

The Pain of Parting; the Joy of Coming Home

Abdul was comforted by the knowledge that as a Christian he was already participating in being a child of God. And later that relationship would mean that he would be welcomed into God's house as a family member. This life and the life to follow are not clearly separated for Christians. It is the coming life that is promised to us which gives meaning, comfort and purpose to this life.

Sometimes those who refuse to commit themselves to Jesus are quick to accuse people who do of escapism—of being so heavenly minded that they're no earthly good. C. S. Lewis suggests that

[The] Christians who did most for the present world were just those who thought most of the next. The Apostles themselves, who set on foot the conversion of the Roman Empire, the great men who built up the Middle Ages, the English Evangelicals who abolished the slave trade, all left their mark on Earth, precisely because their minds were occupied with Heaven. It is since Christians have largely ceased to think of the other world that they have become so ineffective in this. Aim at Heaven and you will get earth "thrown in"; aim at earth and you will get neither.[1]

We thus see that a pilgrim mentality prepares us for both life and death. With this comes an ambiguity about which to choose. Paul expressed this when he wrote: "For me to live is Christ, and to die is gain. . . . Yet which I shall choose I cannot tell. I am hard pressed between the two. My desire is to depart and be with Christ, for that is far better. But to remain in the flesh is more necessary on your account" (Phil 1:21-24). This is no morbid death wish or desire to escape from the responsibilities of life. Paul is happy to stay because the people he loves need him. But he is also eager to see his Savior face to face—the one who claims his first love.

As members of a family we have the same ambiguity. We learn to love each other and grow dependent on one another in the family circle. Then one is suddenly taken from us. We rejoice that another pilgrim has reached the City, but we also may be devastated over the loss of one we still feel we need. At such times the gentle Shepherd will carry us and comfort us. And we can claim the timeless promise: "God . . . will be with them; [wiping] away every tear from their eyes, and death shall be no more, neither shall there be mourning and crying nor pain any more" (Rev 21:3-4).

Hyman Appelman tells of an old man who sat with his dying wife. Both were in their eighties, and in their long life together they had had eight children. But all had gone to be with the Lord before them. They had no grandchildren. As the husband sat beside the bed, his wife reached out for his hand. "She drew a deep breath and asked, 'John, are the children in?' The great hot, heavy tears rolled down his cheeks as he whispered, 'Yes, darling, they are all in.' He meant that all were in heaven."[2]

Life and death is a family affair. Our tears are wiped away when we have the assurance that our loved ones are waiting for us at the finishing line of the race. While this takes the sting out of death— as it did for the old man—the hurt for most of us is still there. This was my experience when my father served his Lord during the war. He refused to leave his post even when he had the chance to do so and was killed by an enemy bomb. As a young person I clung to the promise of Revelation 21, and God did gradually wipe the tears from my eyes, as well as those of my mother and brothers. Somehow we were all wrapped in that great blanket of God's love and were comforted.

For the first time in my life I became fascinated with the songs and promises of the Lord's return. With my father having gone ahead, I longed for Jesus' coming. Whether the Lord returns in our lifetime is not as important as our yearning and longing to see the One we love.

Over and over the Bible uses the analogy of the bride and bridegroom to help us understand how we are promised in love to Christ. When I was engaged to Bob, I was not hesitant to introduce him as my future husband. It's the same in our relationship to Jesus

Christ. We talk about our future spouse and look forward to the day when the marriage will be fulfilled as Jesus comes for his bride: "Let us rejoice and be glad; let us praise his greatness! For the time has come for the wedding of the Lamb, and his bride has prepared herself for it. . . . Happy are those who have been invited" (Rev 19:7, 9 TEV).

Running the Race and Reaching the Goal

Besides the marriage imagery, looking at life and death as a race to be completed is also a familiar picture in the Bible. What's the point of entering a race if there is no intention of reaching the destination or winning the prize? "So run that you may obtain it," writes Paul. "Every athlete exercises self-control in all things. They do it to receive a perishable wreath, but we an imperishable" (1 Cor 9:24-25).

The writer to the Hebrews also uses athletic imagery when he says, "Let us lay aside every weight, and sin which clings so closely, and let us run with perseverance the race that is set before us, looking to Jesus the pioneer and perfecter of our faith, who for the joy that was set before him endured the cross, despising the shame, and is seated at the right hand of the throne of God" (12:1-2). We have the same destination as Jesus had. Running the race and reaching the goal is part of our identity as his disciples:

He who would valiant be
'Gainst all disaster,
Let him in constancy
Follow the Master.
There's no discouragement
Shall make him once relent
His first avowed intent
To be a pilgrim.

Since, Lord, thou dost defend

Us with Thy Spirit,
We know we at the end
Shall life inherit
Then fancies flee away!
I'll fear not what men say,
I'll labor night and day
To be a pilgrim.[3]

John Bunyan's old hymn was familiar to us as children. We had all read his book, so the imagery was well known. Early in life we had accepted our identity as pilgrims in pilgrim families. We were like Abraham and his family who looked for the "city . . . whose builder and maker is God" (Heb 11:8-10).

Our problem—as modern pilgrim families—is keeping this perspective of being on a journey, of not settling down in our well-built homes as if we are going to live here forever. How can we impart to our children and grandchildren that the *journey* is our home—our temporal home—while we continue toward our eternal home? John Howard Yoder points out that for first-century Christians there was no gap between the present and future reality. For us the same is true. What we do each day is what leads us to where we are going.[4]

In order to impart this truth to our children, perhaps we should use more songs about heaven. It has often been said that the songs people sing reflect their focus in life. As children in China, songs about heaven were very much part of life.

These hymns taught us not to separate the journey from the destination, or the race from the finish line. Finding the right direction is the secret to reaching the goal. Or as C. S. Lewis suggests:

We are not living in a world where all roads are radii of a circle and where all, if followed long enough, will therefore draw gradually nearer and finally meet at the centre: rather in a world where every road, after a few miles, forks into two, and each of those into two again, and at each fork you must make a decision. . . . I think earth if chosen instead of Heaven, will turn out to have been, all along, only a region in Hell: and earth if put second to Heaven, to have been from the beginning a part of Heaven itself.[5]

The Family in the Eternal Chorus

As we discover heaven on earth in our times together in family worship, we learn to focus more and more on the Person who is the way and who gives us our identity. Paradoxically, though we become more sensitive than ever to the "still sad music of humanity" with all its conflict of interests, life for the believer becomes more integrated and unified with the years. We could call it a "gestalt" experience as we gain the insight to see the whole picture from the beginning to the end.

When I think of the songs that describe the City of God, I remember my great-grandfather, Kristian Hanes, singing and playing the organ that now stands in my brother Hakon's house. My great-grandfather often gathered his family around the organ to sing, and then he would put the organ on his wagon and go from farm to farm playing, singing and sharing the good news of God's love.

Then there was my mother's father, the sea captain, who brought his organ on board the sailing ship so he could play and sing during the long days at sea.

My own father tied an organ to the back of a mule so it could make the long journey from the coast to a far-off corner of China where he would serve his God and die. Two hours before the bomb dropped on our home he sat down at that organ and sang with my mother the beloved Norwegian hymn, "Takk, min Gud, for alt som hende." I can see him with his deep bass voice and head thrown back singing with great conviction:

Thanks for prayers that Thou hast answered
Thanks for what Thou dost deny
Thanks for home and thanks for fireside
Thanks for hope, that sweet refrain!
Thanks for joy and thanks for sorrow

Thanks for heavenly peace with Thee!
Thanks for hope in the tomorrow,
Thanks through all eternity![6]

Hours later my father was blending his voice with the eternal chorus. As he entered the Celestial City, I can imagine him experiencing the joy expressed by Bunyan's pilgrim: " 'I see the gate! I see the gate! And men standing to receive us'. . . . They were met on the other side by some of the shining host . . . forming an escort to the King. . . . There was singing and shouting and the sounding of trumpets. And all the bells of the city rang with joy."[7]

That is the triumphant homecoming we can all look forward to. Each step we take now in the right direction brings us closer to the gates of the City. While still on earth, our spirits can soar with the angels, for "in the inner sanctuary of our being we are already beginning to know something of that worship in which the King of heaven dwells."[8]

Our state can be compared to that of an audience, standing on tiptoe waiting for curtain time. While we wait, a breeze blows the curtain apart for a moment and we catch a glimpse of what is to come. That's why Paul wrote: "For the creation waits with eager longing . . . because the creation itself will be set free from its bondage . . . and obtain the glorious liberty of the children of God" (Rom 8:19, 21).

When my mother entered the City, she was in Norway while we were in the Philippines, and I found it very difficult to blend my voice with the heavenly chorus she had joined. Tears flowed like rivers, while the music of my soul was all dammed up within. I did not have the advantage my brother Edvard had of conducting her funeral service. Funerals can be wonderful occasions of rejoicing as the family gathers to sing the favorite songs of the one who sings with us on the other side.

Since I did not have this opportunity to celebrate my mother's homecoming, the larger family of pilgrims in the Philippines came to my rescue and agreed to have a memorial service for my mother, whom they had learned to love when she had visited us there eight years before. The choir of Filipino Christians willingly learned one of her favorite songs in Norwegian which they sang like natives: "Den store, hvite flokk a se, som tusen berge full av sne"—which means:

Behold the host arrayed in white,
Like thousand snowclad mountains bright,
With palms they stand, who are this band
Before the throne of light?
These are the ransomed throng, the same
That from the tribulation came,
And in the flood of Jesus' blood
Are cleansed from guilt and shame.
And now arrayed in robes made white
They God are serving day and night,
And anthems swell where God doth dwell,
Mid angels in the height.[9]

It is natural for Norwegians to compare the great crowd of the redeemed to thousands of snowclad mountain peaks. But since my mother had spent most of her adult life in Asia—sometimes among palm trees—it was fitting that this great triumphant hymn also had the redeemed throng waving their palm branches in praise to Jesus their King. And among the palm trees surrounding our church in Davao City, it was fitting that three hundred fifty Filipino pilgrims turned out to join our little faimly of four in worship—to help us blend our voices in praise with the eternal chorus that Mother had just joined.

As the vision gets brighter the closer we get to the City, the more we will long to sing this song. Since heaven has been called the "homeland of music," each time we worship with joyful singing, we as a family are rehearsing for the great concert we'll be part of soon. And each time, our songs blend with the eternal chorus that is singing praises to the Lamb right now—and will continue through all eternity:

"You are worthy. . . .
For you were killed, and by your death you bought for God
people from every tribe, language, nation, and race.
You have made them a kingdom of priests to serve our God,
and they shall rule on earth."

Again I looked, and I heard angels, thousands and millions of
them! They stood around the throne . . . and sang in a loud voice:

"The Lamb who was killed is worthy
to receive power, wealth, wisdom, and strength,
honor, glory, and praise!"

And I heard every creature in heaven, on earth, in the world
below, and in the sea—all living beings in the universe—and
they were singing:

"To him who sits on the throne
and to the Lamb,
be praise and honor,
glory and might, forever and ever!" . . .
"Amen!" (Rev 5:9-14 TEV)

Notes

Chapter 1: The Family's Journey of Faith

[1]John Bunyan, *The Pilgrim's Progress* (Old Tappan, N.J.: Fleming H. Revell, 1975).

[2]Ibid., pp. 145-46.

[3]Henrik Ibsen, *Peer Gynt*, in *The Guthrie Theater Program Magazine*, ed. Brian Anderson (Minneapolis: MSP Publications, 1983), p. 30.

[4]Ibid., p. 23.

[5]Henrik Ibsen, *Peer Gynt*, trans. Peter Watts (New York: Penguin, 1966).

[6]By William Williams, 1745; trans. Peter Williams and William Williams, 1771.

Chapter 2: Marriage: The Start

[1]M. Scott Peck, *The Road Less Traveled* (New York: Simon and Schuster, 1978), p. 84.

[2]Ibid., p. 88.

[3]Ibid.

[4]Ibid., p. 90.

[5]Ibid., p. 98.

[6]Ibid., pp. 103-4.

[7]Andrew Cherline and Frank Furstenberg, Jr., "The American Family in the Year 2000," *The Futurist*, June 1983, pp. 8-9.

[8]Anne Wilson Schaef, *Women's Reality* (Minneapolis: Winston Press, 1981), pp. 60-61.

[9]Berkeley and Alvera Mickelsen, *Biblical Teachings about Men-Women Relationships*, course outline, p. 3.

[10]Kari Torjesen Malcolm, *Women at the Crossroads* (Downers Grove, Ill.: InterVarsity Press), pp. 35-37.

[11]R. Pierce Beaver, *All Loves Excelling* (Grand Rapids, Mich.: Eerdmans, 1968), p. 116.

Chapter 3: Slowing Us Down: Sex, Power and Money

[1]R.C. Sproul, "The Door Interview," *The Wittenburg Door* 79 (June-July 1984), p. 18.

[2]Warren and Ruth Myers, *How to Be Effective in Prayer* (Colorado Springs: Navpress, 1983), p. 58.

[3]Richard Foster, *Money, Sex and Power* (San Francisco: Harper & Row, 1985). Although Foster's book preceded this one into print, I was thinking about these three barriers to relationships before his book arrived in the stores. Seeing it, I was happy to have confirmation from such a respected source of my conclusions.

[4]Gittin 9:10. See Virginia Mollenkott, *Women, Men and the Bible* (Nashville: Abingdon, 1977), p. 11.

[5]Peter Christen Asbjornsen and Jorgen Moe, *Norwegian Folktales*, trans. Pat Shaw and Carl Norman (New York: Pantheon Books, 1982), p. 115.

[6]Author unknown. This saying was frequently quoted by the missionaries of the China Inland Mission when I was a child.

[7]Merrill F. Unger, *Unger's Bible Handbook* (Chicago: Moody Press, 1966), p. 850.

[8]Eric Gelman and Penelope Wang, "They Live to Buy," *Newsweek* 31 December 1984, p. 28.

[9]Hakon Torjesen, *The Househusband* (Eden Prairie, Minn.: The Garden, 1979), pp. 20-21.

[10]"Teach Your Kids What to Do When You're Not Home," *National Center for Youth and Families Netline* 2, no. 2: 4.

[11]Robert L. Vernon, "Unearthing the Roots of Violence in America," *Christianity Today*, 6 August 1982, p. 31.

[12]"An Age of Affluence Could Destroy Values," *USA Today,* 9 February 1984, p. 8A.

[13]*Philippine News,* No. 29, March 19-25, 1986, p. 4.

Chapter 4: Putting Christ in the Lead

[1]Malcolm Muggeridge, "The Door Interview," *The Wittenburg Door,* October-November 1985, p. 22.

[2]Lynn M. Parent and Neil A. Parent, "Parents: First Preachers of the Word," *Spirituality Today* 36 (Spring 1984): 24.

[3]John White, *Parents in Pain* (Downers Grove, Ill.: InterVarsity Press, 1979).

Chapter 5: Spiritual Disciplines: Building Strength in the Home

[1]Richard Foster, *Celebration of Discipline* (New York: Harper and Row, 1978), p. 171.

[2]Brother Lawrence, *The Practice of the Presence of God,* quoted in Richard Foster, *Meditative Prayer* (Downers Grove: InterVarsity Press, 1983), pp. 22-23.

[3]Henri J. M. Nouwen, *The Genesee Diary* (Garden City, N.Y.: Image Books, 1976), p. 13.

[4]Donald Coggan, Archbishop of Canterbury, quoted in Foster, *Celebration of Discipline,* p. 1.

[5]Margaret Jensen, *First We Have Coffee* (San Bernardino, Calif.: Here's Life, 1982), p. 40.

[6]Dietrich Bonhoeffer, *Life Together,* quoted in Richard Foster, *Celebration of Discipline,* p. 129.

[7]Foster, *Celebration of Discipline,* p. 138.

[8]David Watson, *Called and Committed* (Wheaton, Ill.: Harold Shaw: 1982), p. 40.

[9]Thomas a Kempis, *The Imitation of Christ* (Chicago: Moody Press, 1982), pp. 139-41.

[10]Eugene Peterson, *A Long Obedience in the Same Direction* (Downers Grove, Ill.: InterVarsity Press, 1980), p. 15.

Chapter 6: Nurturing Young Disciples

[1]"Erma in Bomburbia," *TIME,* 2 July 1984, p. 56.

[2]Pp. 21-23.

[3]Vernon, "Roots of Violence," *Christianity Today,* p. 31.

[4]Karen Olness, *Parenting Happy Healthy Children* (Minneapolis: Jeremy Books, 1977), pp. 31-33.

[5]M. Scott Peck, *Road,* pp. 47-48.

[6]Charles P. Warren in "Synopsis of Youth Films," *Life Productions.* Used with permission from writer and producer.

[7]Ruth McNaughton Hinds and Faith McNaughton Lowell, *Who* (Wheaton, Ill.: Scripture Press, 1966).

[8]*Hush: A Songbook for Today's Youth* (Philippines: Goodwill Press, 1972), no. 94.

[9]*Golden Bells* (London: Children's Special Service Mission, 1925), no. 560.

[10]Robert McKewin, *Lordsway Letter,* summer 1984, p. 1.

[11]For a thorough study of spiritual gifts see C. Peter Wagner, *Your Church Can Grow* (Glendale, Calif.: Regal, 1976).

[12]*Golden Bells,* no. 222.

[13]Michael Omartian and Stormie Omartian, "Overcoming Painful Childhoods," *Focus on the Family,* March/April 1983, p. 2.

[14]Olli Valtonen, "The Kingdom Call to the World," taped sermon from the Lutheran Conference on the Holy Spirit, 1983.

Chapter 7: The Big Issues of Growing Up

[1]*Golden Bells,* no. 683.

[2]Bruno V. Manno, "After the Fall: The Teen's Search for Self," *Marriage and Family Living,* March 1985, p. 17.

[3]Kathleen Winkler, "Is Rock Music Bruising Your Children?" *Marriage and Family Living,* March 1985, pp. 14-15.

[4]"Undercover," *The Wittenburg Door,* October-November 1984, p. 24.

[5]Keith Green, "So you wanna go to Egypt," Pretty Good Records-1. Produced by Bill Maxwell and Keith Green, 1980, Last Day Ministries.

[6]M. Basilea Schlink, "Christians and Rock Music," *The Plough,* May-June 1985, pp. 8-10.

[7]David Watson, *Called and Committed* (Wheaton: Harold Shaw, 1982), p. 125.

[8]Clyde Kilby, *Images of Salvation in the Fiction of C. S. Lewis* (Wheaton: Harold Shaw, 1978), p. 54.

Chapter 8: Our Extended Family

[1]Parker J. Palmer, *A Place Called Community,* Pendlehill Pamphlet 212, 1977, p. 22.

[2]*Songs* (San Anselmo, Calif.: Songs and Creations), p. 14, permission requested.

Chapter 9: Reaching beyond the Home

[1]Michael Green, *Evangelism in the Early Church* (Grand Rapids: Eerdmans, 1970), p. 219.

[2]Ibid.

[3]Ibid., p. 220.

[4]Ibid., pp. 221-22.

[5]Ibid., p. 228.

[6]Ibid., pp. 218-19.

[7]Ibid., pp. 250-51, 249.

[8]Doloros R. Leckey, *The Ordinary Way: A Family Spirituality* (New York: Crossroad, 1982), p. 5.

Chapter 10: Journey's End

[1]C. S. Lewis, *Mere Christianity* (New York: Macmillan, 1952), p. 116.

[2]Hyman J. Appelman, *Will the Circle Be Unbroken?* (Grand Rapids: Zondervan, 1948), pp. 18-19.

[3]*Golden Bells,* no. 522.

[4]John Howard Yoder, *The Politics of Jesus* (Grand Rapids, Mich.: Eerdmans, 1972), p. 249.

[5]C. S. Lewis, *The Great Divorce* (Grand Rapids, Mich.: Baker Book House, 1969), pp. 111-12.

[6]*Gospel Hymnal* (Chicago: Baptist Conference Press, 1950), no. 270.

[7]John Bunyan, quoted in Robert E. Coleman, *Songs of Heaven* (Old Tappan, N.J.: Revell, 1980), p. 158.

[8]Ibid.

[9]*Mike and Else's Norwegian Songbook* (Minneapolis: Skandisk Publications, 1985), no. 86.